India vs Pakistan

India vs Pakistan

Why Can't We Just Be Friends?

Husain Haqqani

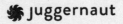

JUGGERNAUT BOOKS

KS House, 118 Shahpur Jat, New Delhi 110049, India

First published by Juggernaut Books 2016

ISBN 9788193237250

Typeset in Adobe Caslon Pro by R. Ajith Kumar, New Delhi

Printed at Manipal Technologies Ltd

Contents

1

'We Can Either Be More Than Friends or Become More Than Enemies'

Barely seven months after Pakistan's creation, Pakistan's founder, Muhammad Ali Jinnah, and the US ambassador to the new country, Paul Alling, met for tea at a beach cottage on the shores of the Arabian Sea, a few miles from Karachi. As the two strolled along the sandy beach in the spring sun Jinnah declared that 'nothing was dearer to his heart' than close relations between India and Pakistan. Jinnah said he sincerely wished for India and Pakistan to have 'an association similar to that between the United States and Canada'. Alling informed Washington in a diplomatic telegram that Jinnah spoke of Pakistan's 'defensive understanding with India on a military level' with no time limit. This would resemble American arrangements with Canada, which allow the two neighbours to have largely unguarded borders, shared defence, free trade and freedom of movement through several crossing points.[1]

Through the remaining months of his life, Jinnah continuously held out the promise of friendly relations between the two dominions carved out of British India. He had not anticipated the violence that accompanied Partition, fed by the rhetoric of the All India Muslim League, the Hindu Mahasabha and the Akali Dal. Earlier in his career, in 1917, he had been described by Sarojini Naidu as 'the ambassador of Hindu–Muslim unity'.

His decision to form Pakistan had never been communal, at least in his view. As a lawyer and politician, Jinnah was known for the cold, calm and detached manner in which he examined and addressed issues. Once he embraced the two-nation theory – the idea that India's Muslims were a separate nation from Hindus by virtue of their religion, culture and historic experience – Jinnah 'virtually conjured' Pakistan 'into statehood by the force of his indomitable will'.[2] As his biographer Stanley Wolpert observed:

Few individuals significantly alter the course of history.

Fewer still modify the map of the world. Hardly anyone can be credited with creating a nation-state. Mohammad Ali Jinnah did all three.[3]

Having created Pakistan out of communal friction, Jinnah realized that it could not be a nation mired in religious strife forever. He stressed secularism, as opposed to theocracy, as the ideal for Pakistan.

Jinnah was also keen for India and Pakistan not to be in a state of permanent war. Hence, his avowal of the desire for relations similar to those between Canada and the United States. That Jinnah did not envisage Pakistan's permanent enmity with India is borne out also by his wish to return to his Mumbai home after retirement as Governor-General of Pakistan.

India's Bapu, Mohandas Karamchand Gandhi, was no less enthusiastic about good ties between the two countries that he believed had been born through an 'agreed separation between brothers'.[4] Unlike Jinnah, Gandhi had been passionately against Partition, arguing that different religions did not create nationality. But once

Partition had been effected, Gandhi cautioned against India and Pakistan becoming 'perpetual enemies'. The two independent countries, he had warned, had to 'live as friends or die as such'.

Sixty-nine years and four wars later, Jinnah and Gandhi's vision seems like a blur. When they are not engaged in direct hostilities, the two countries – both now armed with nuclear weapons – seem embroiled in a cold war. Over the last several years, their leaders have been meeting every now and then, usually on the sidelines of an international summit, and announcing resumption of talks at the level of officials. Within a few days, a terrorist attack in India that is traced to a Pakistan-based jihadi group breaks the momentum for dialogue, or there are allegations of ceasefire violations along the Line of Control in Jammu and Kashmir.

For decades, Pakistan has accused India of supporting ethnic separatism on its soil, even as India charges Pakistan with sponsoring terrorism in India and beyond. India–Pakistan talks get derailed, often only to be resumed with much fanfare until the next round of terrorist attacks, accusations, and cancellation or postponement of talks. Whether they choose to use the word or not, significant numbers of Indians and Pakistanis view each other as enemies rather than as brothers separated by circumstances.

The two states born out of the Partition of British India might still be able to live amicably with one another, but prospects of that can best be described as distant, at least right now. Seven decades of separation have created issues and bred psychoses that make it difficult for most people to even remember the unities of the preceding centuries. But why this enmity? And who is to blame? In this book I argue that the responsibility for the present state of affairs lies on both sides of the border (and occasionally third parties), but that it has especially been made tangled by Pakistan's near pathological obsession with India.

The tensions between the countries were seeded early. Jinnah's conciliatory approach was not shared by many in the Muslim League nor by Pakistan's civil and military bureaucracy who saw advantage in maintaining the frenzy of Partition while they consolidated control over the new country. The unwillingness of India's government leaders, notably Prime Minister Jawaharlal Nehru and Home Minister Sardar Vallabhbhai Patel, to be generous to the new state, especially in the division of assets, also made reconciliation difficult.

In his first address to Pakistan's Constituent Assembly on 11 August 1947, Jinnah said that he saw Partition as a 'mighty revolution' that had resolved 'India's constitutional problem' of one religious community being in majority and another being a minority. His vision had borne fruit. It was now time for 'co-operation, forgetting the past, burying the hatchet'.[5] But that was easier said than done.

In India, Jinnah's shiny optimism about Pakistan was not necessarily shared. The Congress had vehemently opposed Partition. Even the All India Congress Committee (AICC) resolution that approved Mountbatten's 3 June 1947 Partition plan described it as only a temporary solution. It expressed the hope that after the subsiding of 'present passions' India's problems would be viewed in their proper perspective and 'the false doctrine of two-nations will be discredited and discarded by all'.[6]

The Congress resolution also reaffirmed the territorial unity of the Indian subcontinent – 'Geography and the

mountains and the seas fashioned India as she is ...
Economic circumstances and the insistent demands of
international affairs make the unity of India still more
necessary. The picture of India we have learnt to cherish
will remain in our minds and in our hearts.'[7]

Pakistanis have often interpreted the resolution and
other similar statements to mean that India wanted to
actively undo Partition. From the start, Pakistan's elite
started mixing legitimate concerns about security with
huge doses of paranoia. It also did not help that the
communal riots accompanying Partition resulted in at
least half a million deaths and 10–14.5 million refugees,
Muslims moving to Pakistan and Hindus and Sikhs to
India.[8] Every community involved in the mayhem blamed
others instead of taking responsibility for its own share in
the viciousness. Those affected by the Partition violence in
each country became a constituency for anger, bitterness
and hostility towards the other. In Pakistan's case that
included most of its early political leaders, senior civil
servants and many military officers.

But Nehru also did little to allay these fears, often
saying contradictory things in the early years after

Independence. On one hand the Indian prime minister seemed to share Jinnah's vision that the two countries could maintain their separate identities and still be close. 'Nothing can overcome the basic urges, historical, cultural and economic, that tend to bring us nearer to each other,' he asserted.

But in Pakistan, such sentiments were understood quite differently. All references to the shared heritage of India and Pakistan were deemed an attack on the very foundation of Pakistan, a scheme to erode Pakistan's identity as a separate nation.

In a speech at Aligarh Muslim University in January 1948, Nehru tried to reassure Pakistan that India did not question Pakistan's right to exist as a separate country. 'If today by any chance I were offered the reunion of India and Pakistan,' he said, 'I would decline it for obvious reasons. I do not want to carry the burden of Pakistan's great problems. I have enough of my own. Any closer association must come out of a normal process and in a friendly way which does not end Pakistan as a State, but makes it an equal part of a larger union in which several countries might be associated.'⁹

None of these assurances really helped calm Pakistan's ruling elite. They continued to believe during this period that India's ultimate strategic objective was to reabsorb Pakistan. Before Partition, the Indian National Congress and the All India Muslim League had a lively political rivalry, constantly trying to outmanoeuvre each other. These politics had spilled over into India–Pakistan relations.

But it wasn't all paranoia and lack of trust on Pakistan's part. Nehru's words did not always translate into action. Gandhi proposed that Pakistan be treated like members of a family who had moved out of a joint family to their own home; Pakistanis needed to be won over, not cut off further from their estranged clan. Nehru and his powerful Home Minister Sardar Vallabhbhai Patel, however, treated Pakistan more with the disdain that Mughal emperors showed towards their renegade provinces, never missing an opportunity to point out the 'error' of dividing the subcontinent, possibly at the behest of the British.

Patel publicly doubted Pakistan's prospects of survival as a separate country, insisting that 'Sooner than later we shall again be united in common allegiance to our country', an unambiguous reference to undivided India. He also reminded Indians before his death in December 1950, 'Do not forget that important limbs of your Mother India have been cut.'[10]

India's Pakistan policy in those early years was also influenced by political priorities at home, such as reassuring angry Hindus and Sikhs displaced from Pakistan, keeping Hindu (as opposed to Indian) nationalism at bay and winning over India's Muslims to the Congress.

With Muslim-majority provinces separated from the Indian Union, Nehru focused on transforming the Congress from a national independence movement to a ruling political party in the world's most populous democracy. India's Muslim minority, many of whom had supported Jinnah and the Muslim League during the twilight of the British Raj, had been left leaderless after Partition.

The Congress could now tap India's Muslims as a vote bank if it could convince them that they had been abandoned. They did this continually, reminding the community that they would have been better off had

Pakistan not been created. Overseas, India's diplomats rejected the logic of Partition in competition with their Pakistani counterparts, who were struggling to introduce their new nation on the world stage. For most Pakistanis, this attitude deepened their mistrust of India, and reinforced the reasons that had led to the demand for Pakistan in the first place.

Pakistan too was creating its own narratives in these early days of nation-building – some of it fuelling anti-India feeling. The politicians in charge of the new country were migrants from India, and not indigenous to the region that was now Pakistan. This made them highlight an ideological Pakistan with which their association could be more easily established. They emphasized the two-nation theory and the notion of an eternal conflict between Hindus and Muslims.

For example, Prime Minister Liaquat Ali Khan, nawabzada of a minor princely state in Haryana, declared repeatedly that Pakistan was to be 'a country where the Islamic principles could be applied, where the Muslims could live according to their own genius'.[11] Similar views were expressed by ministers who had migrated from

India as well as by the head of the civil service, Chaudhry Muhammad Ali, who came from Jalandhar.

Describing Pakistan as a citadel of Islam and defining 'Hindu India' as the 'other' to a 'Muslim Pakistan' were easy diversions from questions about why people who were born in and had spent their entire lives in the United Provinces, Delhi, Bombay or Calcutta were now running a country which did not include those places.

The Pashtun leader Abdul Ghaffar Khan, known as the 'Frontier Gandhi', had supported the Congress and led it in 1946 to secure more Muslim votes than the Muslim League in the Northwest Frontier Province (now known as Khyber-Pashtunkhwa). After Independence, Ghaffar Khan complained that Pakistan's rulers, most of whom were not sons of the soil, sought to keep the Pakistani people under control by making them live in a nightmare of riots, assaults, and '"holy" war'.[12] Ghulam Murtaza Syed, a prominent Sindhi, criticized the 'planned colonization' of his province through the 'heavy influx of alien people in Sindh', a reference to Punjabis and Urdu-speaking Muhajirs who moved in after Partition.[13]

The emphasis on a religion-based 'ideology of Pakistan'

did not dampen the ethnic differences within Pakistan. It did, however, fuel hatred and animosity, which has made normal relations with India difficult.

To complicate matters further, Pakistan's share out of Partition comprised 21 per cent of British India's population[14] and 17 per cent of its revenue but as much as one-third of the large armed forces that had been raised by the British during the Second World War.

The British policy of considering certain ethnic groups and communities in India as 'martial races' had favoured recruitment of Pashtun and Punjabi Muslims whose homeland was now part of Pakistan. Under the terms of Partition, Pakistan received 30 per cent of British India's army, 40 per cent of its navy and 20 per cent of its air force.[15] Prime Minister Liaquat Ali Khan was forced in 1948 to allocate 75 per cent of Pakistan's first budget to cover the salaries and maintenance costs of this huge force.[16]

Thus, Pakistan was not like other countries that raise an army to deal with threats they face; it had inherited a large army that needed a threat if it was to be maintained. Although India's army was twice the size of Pakistan's, the country's size and revenue base was larger and India could cite several potential sources of threat to justify its armed forces. In Pakistan's case, the only threat that could be invoked to retain the legions inherited from the Raj was India.

The Pakistan army's first two commanders-in-chief were British generals. When the first Muslim commander-in-chief, General Ayub Khan, assumed the military's leadership he spoke of how 'Brahmin chauvinism and arrogance' had led to Pakistan's creation.[17] Ayub and other generals argued that Pakistan needed a large military to protect itself against Hindu India.

They claimed the Hindus wanted to avenge seven centuries of Muslim rule over the subcontinent by menacing Muslim Pakistan. Ayub even declared that India had 'a deep pathological hatred for Muslims' and that its hostility to Pakistan stemmed from its 'refusal to see a Muslim power developing next door'.[18]

Ironically, the real threats to Pakistan at the time of its inception stemmed from economic and political factors, not military ones. The Partition plan of 3 June 1947 had given only seventy-two days for transition to

Independence. But Pakistan, unlike India, did not have a functioning capital, central government or financial resources. The Muslim League leaders had done little homework to prepare for running the country they had demanded.

Within days of Independence, Pakistan was concerned about its share of India's assets, both financial and military. It was also caught without a concrete plan to deal with negotiating the accession of princely states, fourteen of whom (out of 562) had Muslim-majority populations and were contiguous to or located within the territory of Pakistan.

The Muslim League's lack of preparation meant that on the day of Pakistan's independence, only one of these states, Swat, had joined the new Muslim dominion. This contrasted with India's ability to integrate by Independence Day all but six of the 548 princely states that became part of the Indian Union. Thus, Pakistan's territory remained undefined for several months after Independence. The princely states in Pakistan eventually fell in line while one – Kalat, in Balochistan – was coerced through military action in March 1948.

17

Moreover, at inception, Pakistan comprised two wings separated by a thousand miles of Indian territory. Creating a system of governance that would satisfy the Bengalis of East Pakistan and Punjabi-dominated West Pakistan was a tall order. Getting the new state on its feet economically was another major challenge. Pakistan had virtually no industry and the major markets for its agricultural products were in India. Pakistan produced 75 per cent of the world's jute supply but did not have a single jute-processing mill. All the mills were in India. Although one-third of undivided India's cotton was grown in Pakistan, it had only one-thirtieth of the cotton mills.[19]

The non-Muslim entrepreneurial class, which had dominated commerce in the areas now constituting Pakistan, had either fled or transferred its capital across the new border. Uncertainties about Pakistan's survival may have partly been the reason for flight of capital, but for the new country's leaders it was a 'Hindu conspiracy' to economically strangulate Pakistan. The country's revenue base had shrunk even further than the 17 per cent it would have been if the Partition had proceeded smoothly and

Pakistan had received everything it was allocated under the terms of the division.

Pakistan's economic crisis was made worse by the threat of political chaos. The larger idea that had united diverse Muslim supporters of Pakistan's creation could no longer be maintained now that the country had come into being. While Jinnah was concerned about containing the communal violence already stoked during Partition, his successors (he died in September 1948, barely a year after Pakistan came into being) decided that the religious passions could also be used for consolidating Pakistan's nationhood and their own power.

One of the major arguments advanced for an independent Pakistan had been the notion that, irrespective of population, Hindus and Muslims should be treated as two separate and equal nations. The Muslim League referred to this demand as the doctrine of parity. Now that Pakistan had come into existence, its economic and military disparity with India was obvious. Pakistan was India's sovereign equal in terms of international law but the two countries could not be uniform in terms of their military strength or international stature.

This reality, however, did not matter to Pakistani politicians struggling to create a support base at home. The Pakistani military realized that it would have to effectively control the country to be able to get the lion's share of its resources. Pursuit of military parity with India could justify forever greater allocation of resources to the military. It was in the military's institutional interest to encourage Pakistan's evolution as a national security state, living in constant fear of being overrun by an India that had not reconciled to its existence.

Barely seven months after Independence, the Bengali leader Huseyn Shaheed Suhrawardy warned Pakistan's Constituent Assembly that Pakistan was on a perilous course. As chief minister of undivided Bengal, Suhrawardy had witnessed the horrors of communal violence, and had aided the Muslim League in creating the Hindu–Muslim polarization that helped it win Muslim votes for Pakistan. But that was a different time requiring different politics. 'Now,' he said, addressing Pakistan's government, 'you are raising the cry of Pakistan in danger for the purpose of arousing Muslim sentiments and binding them together in order to maintain you in power.'[20]

Suhrawardy, briefly Pakistan's prime minister in 1956, warned against Pakistan becoming 'a state which will be founded on sentiments, namely that of Islam in danger or of Pakistan in danger'. He foresaw that the Muslim League leaders were making Pakistan 'a state which will be held together by raising the bogey of attacks', and which would be kept together by encouraging 'constant friction' between Pakistan and its 'sister dominion' India. 'That state,' Suhrawardy cautioned, 'will be full of alarms and excursions.'

Pakistan continued to nurture a national narrative of grievance against India, its military gained further prominence once the country joined western anti-communist alliances, Kashmir became a bone of contention between the two states and the commonalities that bound India and Pakistan began to be deliberately erased as Pakistan attempted to draw closer to the Arab Middle East.

Pakistan's lack of preparation in dealing with princely states contributed to the creation of a major flashpoint for perennial India–Pakistan conflict. The largest Muslim-majority princely state, Jammu and Kashmir, posed a problem for at least three reasons: First, it adjoined both India and Pakistan; second, its Hindu maharaja, Hari Singh, initially flirted with remaining independent; and third, its popular Muslim political leader, Sheikh Abdullah, was closer to the Congress than to the Muslim League.

Pakistan tried to strengthen its hand in Jammu and Kashmir with the help of armed volunteers, recruited from among Pashtun tribesmen. This in turn paved the way for India's direct military involvement. The Muslim League had missed the boat on winning Sheikh Abdullah over, but Pakistan could have built on a Standstill Agreement it signed with Maharaja Hari Singh and sought his accession to Pakistan. By launching an ill-planned tribal invasion, Pakistan drove the maharaja into India's arms. Initiating a war and losing it is not the optimal way of starting life as a new country. The use of force eroded Pakistan's moral argument about Kashmir belonging to Pakistan by virtue of its Muslim majority.

For some the dispute over Kashmir was a godsend. Patel, already unfavourably disposed to Pakistan, argued that Pakistan was now virtually at war with India and no country could be expected to arm or fund an adversary in the middle of war. This resulted in India withholding Pakistan's share of assets located in India due to them under the Partition scheme. This accentuated the acrimony of Partition.

Pakistan was allocated a 17.5 per cent share in the assets and liabilities of British India. Cash balances were held by the Reserve Bank of India (RBI), which held back the transfer of 750 million rupees for months. Fighting in Kashmir jeopardized Pakistan's share of 165,000 tons of arms, ammunition and other military material – by 31 March 1948 India had transferred only 4730 tons and another 18,000 tons by 10 September 1948. To this day, Pakistanis assert that India held 1,42,000 tons of defence stores that should have come to Pakistan.

A similar motive was attributed to India's decision in April 1948 to cut off the supply of water from two headworks of the Punjab canal system under its control. In the autumn of 1947 the chief engineers of India and Pakistan had signed a Standstill Agreement which froze water allocations until 31 March 1948. India discontinued the delivery of water to two major canals for a month on the day that the Standstill Agreement expired, demanding a new permanent agreement. The delivery of water was resumed a month later after an Inter-Dominion conference and India agreed it would not withdraw water delivery without allowing time for Pakistan to develop alternative sources. Pakistan's leaders, however, saw this not as a technical matter, but as part of India's plan to cripple agriculture in Pakistan.

Gandhi recognized the importance of containing the sourness in India–Pakistan relations when he went on a fast in January 1948 and demanded that Pakistan's share of the monetary assets be paid immediately.[21] That did not assuage the Pakistani sentiment. The country was now fixated on victimhood and India was to be seen as the principal victimizer. For example, it was argued that the boundary in Punjab had deliberately been drawn in a way that provided India access to Kashmir by land. Although Pakistan had played its cards poorly in securing accession of Kashmir, the loss of the Muslim-majority state was attributed to a British–Indian conspiracy rather than poor planning on the part of the Muslim League. Kashmir was now a casus belli and India and Pakistan were in a state of war from their birth as modern independent states.

Still, for almost a decade after Partition, travel between India and Pakistan was relatively easy. The railroads built by the British carried large number of visitors in both directions. Until 1951, when Pakistan formalized its citizenship law, Muslims from India could travel back and forth, looking for better prospects. They did not require a passport, which was not introduced until June 1952.[22] Even then, an India–Pakistan passport, valid only for travel between the two countries, was issued before being replaced by international passports that became necessary only after 1965. Visa requirements also came into effect then, a full eighteen years after Partition.

Films and publications from either country were marketed freely in the other. Urdu poets went across for mushairas, sports exchanges were frequent and trade continued despite limitations imposed by different currency and customs regulations. Civilian politicians and civil servants on either side of the border often knew each other, while newspaper editors and professors interacted frequently.

The freedom of movement and ambiguity in citizenship

laws of the early years created some interesting situations. Pakistan nominated Mohammad Ismail, a UP Muslim who had not physically migrated to Pakistan, as its first high commissioner to India. Controversy arose when the *Tanvir* newspaper in Lucknow reported that the Pakistani high commissioner considered himself an Indian and had no intention of adopting Pakistani nationality.[23] Ismail could not serve as high commissioner and receive diplomatic immunity while remaining a citizen of the country where he was accredited. He, and many Muslim League leaders in Muslim-minority provinces, had assumed that they could continue to live on their estates and own property in India while representing Pakistan.

Some Muslim public figures went back and forth for a couple of years before making a final choice of citizenship. Among them was Chaudhry Khaliq-uz-Zaman, also from UP, who was leader of the opposition in India's Constituent Assembly before finally settling down in Karachi and becoming president of the Pakistan Muslim League. Uncertainty about nationality was not limited to Muslim Leaguers. Jogendar Nath Mandal, a Bengali Scheduled Caste leader, crossed over in 1947 to become

Pakistan's law minister at Jinnah's invitation, but returned to Calcutta in 1950. UP-born Sajjad Zaheer served as leader of the Pakistan Communist Party immediately after Independence and was arrested in 1951 on charges of sedition, only to be deported three years later to India after claiming Indian citizenship.

———

Things began to change dramatically with Pakistan's first military coup in 1958. The army had started wielding political influence as soon as the first native commander, General (later Field Marshal) Ayub Khan, took over from British generals in 1951, the same year that Pakistan's first prime minister, Liaquat Ali Khan, was assassinated. Ayub had trained as a native military officer in the British Indian army and was promoted despite not being 'in the highest intellectual class' and his 'failure as commanding officer' during the Second World War. His British commanding officer who anticipated Partition, however, appreciated Ayub's 'great admiration for British Army methods' and thought Pakistan could use a senior Muslim officer of

Ayub's disposition after the departure of the British.[24]

Ayub did not have a political mind and his views on Pakistan's politics were shaped by the simple question 'What is good for the army?' He remained commander for seven years, with several changes of prime ministers in between, before directly taking power and rewriting the Constitution. Under Ayub's stewardship, the army became exalted as the institution defining Pakistan's national interest. By toppling a civilian leader, Ayub also set a precedent for military intervention in Pakistan's politics timed to halt normalization of India–Pakistan relations. Before Ayub's coup in October 1958, for example, Prime Minister Firoz Khan Noon had spoken of 'the folly of war' with India, only to be ridiculed by the Muslim League and the Islamist Jamaat-e-Islami who called for use of force to settle India–Pakistan issues.

As an Anglophile and staunch ally of the United States, Ayub garnered considerable international influence for Pakistan. India, under Nehru, had chosen to remain non-aligned in the Cold War, and Pakistan benefited from that decision by seeking arms and aid from the US, which helped it maintain military parity with India.

28

For years, the Americans did not realize that enrolling Pakistan as a partner in global strategic ventures buttressed conflict in South Asia. The US provided Pakistan weapons and training, ostensibly to fight international communism even though Pakistan wanted these for its competition with India. Having American backing discouraged Pakistan from negotiating directly with the Indians.

By 1963, thanks to US funding and weapons, Pakistan's military had become twice as large as it was at Partition. Pakistan's army had advanced Patton tanks while its air force flew sophisticated F-86 Sabre jets. Some Pakistani generals felt they could now flex muscle against India and settle the dispute over Kashmir. India had only recently had its nose bloodied in the war with China in 1962, and Nehru's death in 1964 gave Ayub the confidence that Pakistan would have the upper hand in a military engagement against an India lacking a towering figure as prime minister.

Pakistan initiated hostilities in 1965 by sending infiltrators into Kashmir. Its expectation that the Kashmiri Muslims would arise in mass rebellion against India, in support of Pakistan, was not fulfilled. On 6 September 1965 India retaliated for Pakistan's foray into Kashmir by widening the war along Pakistan's international border. The US suspended supplies of arms to both India and Pakistan, causing massive disappointment in Pakistan. The war ended in a stalemate, denying Pakistan the military advantage it had hoped for. Both militaries returned to their pre-war positions after talks brokered by the Soviet Union at Tashkent. Pakistan had tried and failed to wrest Jammu and Kashmir by force. India could not conquer the city of Lahore and did not attack East Pakistan, which was virtually undefended. Both sides had fought to gain nothing, territorially or politically.

The Pakistanis lost 3000–5000 men and about 250 tanks and fifty aircraft, whereas the casualties on the Indian side were greater – 4000–6000 men, about 300 tanks and fifty aircraft. With their much larger population and bigger army, the Indians were better able to absorb these losses.[25] Pakistan occupied 1600 square miles of Indian territory, 1300 of it in the desert, while India secured 350 square miles of Pakistani real estate in Punjab and Kashmir. Pakistanis could take some comfort in having held off a much larger force but as the party that started the war, they had little to show for it.

If anything, that the war was a draw, with victory for neither side, should have alerted leaders in both countries to the futility of confrontation. Nehru had once warned Indians and Pakistanis that 'Because of our very close contacts we cannot be indifferent to each other. We can either be more than friends or become more than enemies.'[26] With soldiers from both sides killed, injured and taken prisoners of war and citizens having experienced bombing raids by the other's air force, the 1965 war left India and Pakistan seeing each other as more than enemies.

The war ended the era of relatively free travel across the border. Exchange of films, books and magazines ended, as did trade. Jingoistic rhetoric unleashed from both sides opened old wounds and inflicted new ones that could not be easily healed. Ramachandra Guha writes of 'a surge of patriotism' that overcame the population of New Delhi. Newsmen spoke of the fall of Lahore as if the Pakistanis were incapable of resisting the Indian army even though Lahore never fell.[27]

In Pakistan religious symbolism and calls to jihad were used to build the morale of soldiers and the people. On the first day of India's offensive against the Pakistan border, Ayub Khan addressed the nation and set the tone for the India–Pakistani relationship for years to come: '… Indian aggression in Kashmir was only a preparation for an attack on Pakistan. Today [the Indians] have given final proof of this.' Ayub cited 'the evil intentions, which India has always harbored against Pakistan since its inception', blaming the war on Hindus' 'customary cowardice and hypocrisy'. Calling for jihad, he declared, 'The 100 million people of Pakistan whose hearts beat with the sound of "La ilaha illallah, Muhammad Ur Rasool Ullah" [There is no God but God and Muhammad is His messenger] will not rest till India's guns are silenced.'[28]

The Pakistani media ran stories of unusual gallantry, of divine help and superhuman resistance alongside tales of Indian cowardice. The story of dedicated soldiers who served as live mines and committed suicide to blow up the advancing Indian tanks in the Sialkot sector became a popular war legend. Both soldiers and civilians reported seeing with their own eyes 'green-robed angels deflecting bombs from their targets – bridges, culverts, mosques – with a wave of the hand. Soldiers were reported shooting enemy aircraft with their .303s [rifles].'[29] During and after the war, Pakistan's official propaganda made the case that one Muslim soldier had the fighting prowess to subdue five Hindus.

The result of cultivating jingoism was that barely six years after their futile war, India and Pakistan were at war again. This time it was in East Pakistan and it was far more decisive than the earlier encounter.

Pakistan's military regime, under General Yahya Khan, had organized the country's first direct election in December 1970, only to find that the Bengalis of East Pakistan voted overwhelmingly for a party – Awami League – that was unacceptable to the military because of its opposition to central rule, demands for greater provincial autonomy, support for secularism and calls for normal relations with India. As East Pakistan accounted for a majority of Pakistan's population, an electoral sweep by the Awami League gave it a clear majority in the new Constituent Assembly. The army refused to hand power over to the Bengali leaders, the people of East Pakistan came out in open rebellion and the military tried to suppress the Bengali revolt by force.

India sided with the Bengali people, citing concerns about the large numbers of refugees pouring across its borders. Pakistan accused India of trying to dismember Pakistan by supporting Bengalis. Outnumbered and isolated from its headquarters, Pakistan's Eastern Command surrendered to the joint forces of India and Bangladesh in December 1971, and 93,000 Pakistanis became prisoners of war. Pakistan was reduced to its erstwhile western wing after the rest of the world followed India in recognizing the new state of Bangladesh.

If a stalemated war failed to persuade the protagonists of the need to give up their animosity, could a war that resulted in conclusive defeat for one and glorious victory for the other do so? India expected a defeated and humiliated Pakistan, shorn of half its territory and more than half its population, to be more deferential and less belligerent than before. But Zulfikar Ali Bhutto, who would lead Pakistan's civilian government for the next five years, put the onus of friendly relations on India.

'India must act with magnanimity,' he told US Secretary of State William Rogers two days after the surrender of Pakistani forces at Dhaka and before flying back to Pakistan to take power.

Bhutto wanted the Indians to understand that he would need time to prepare Pakistani public opinion for 'what has taken place'. Even in this moment of Pakistan's defeat, Bhutto's anti-India nationalism trumped pragmatism. He wanted India to act with humility at a time of Pakistani humiliation and declared that Indians lacked vision when it came to dealing with Pakistan. India, he said, had a 'glorious opportunity either to seek reconciliation with Pakistan or become enemy of Pakistan, for all time on [a] scale like Carthage and Rome'. He predicted 'hatred for all time, utter chaos and terrible massacre' if India missed this opportunity to reconcile. Reconciliation here most likely meant accepting Pakistan's demands even when Pakistan had been decisively defeated in a military encounter.

Moreover, within days of taking over the reins of power in what was left of Pakistan, Bhutto was already working on rebuilding Pakistan's military. In doing so, he hoped to win the favour of Pakistan's generals forever, forestalling the prospects of future military coups – an expectation that was not fulfilled.

Bhutto was charismatic, intelligent, well-educated and eloquent. He became a polarizing figure in Pakistani politics. What his supporters saw as flexibility and pragmatism was unscrupulousness and opportunism to his critics. His admirers loved his exuberant self-confidence, which his opponents termed as arrogance. As the scion of a landowning Sindhi family, Bhutto had grown up during the independence movement in a political family. His father had served as premier of Sindh and diwan in the state of Junagadh. Like many Muslims studying in Mumbai at the time, Bhutto embraced Jinnah's two-nation theory and carried those ideas with him as he went on for higher education at Oxford and the University of California, Berkeley.

Like Jinnah as well as other Pakistanis of his generation, Bhutto was culturally liberal but politically committed to religious nationalism. As a minister in Ayub's military regime, he was identified as a strong proponent of war to secure Kashmir, in addition to being viewed as a hardliner against India. It was nothing short of an irony that it was Bhutto's task to negotiate with India after Pakistan's disastrous war over Bangladesh.

When Bhutto and Indian Prime Minister Indira Gandhi met in the summer of 1972 at Shimla, it was hardly a meeting of equals. Bhutto had to negotiate the release of Pakistani POWs, secure the return of 5139 square miles of Pakistani territory occupied by India and figure out a way to reconcile with the loss of Bangladesh. From India's perspective this was the moment to finally resolve the dispute over Jammu and Kashmir and get Pakistan to give up on notions of parity with India.

Bhutto told Indira Gandhi that Pakistan's domestic political situation did not allow him to sign a treaty settling the argument over Kashmir forever and the Pakistani military would not accept, even in defeat, an explicit no-war pact. Radical opinions would gain popularity in Pakistan, he argued, that would accuse him of losing Kashmir in addition to East Pakistan. Bhutto pleaded for the middle ground, suggesting that de-escalation of tensions take place in stages. He could always return a few years later with a stronger hand at home in order to deal with the deeper sources of conflict.

Bhutto later took credit for saving Pakistan at the Shimla negotiations from the ultimate capitulation of completely giving up its claim on Kashmir.[30] Against the advice of some of her officials, Indira Gandhi accepted Bhutto's argument. Although she distrusted Bhutto, she saw him as preferable to a successor military regime. For India, domestic unrest or the balkanization of Pakistan, with its impact spreading to neighbouring countries, would not be a favourable development. The compromise was to declare that 'the two countries are resolved to settle their differences by peaceful means through bilateral negotiations'. This effectively precluded war.

The ceasefire line in Jammu and Kashmir was declared the Line of Control (LOC). Indian signatories interpreted this to mean that actual control was now synonymous with legal possession. Pakistani prisoners of war returned home, vowing to avenge the loss of East Pakistan as they rejoined the ranks of an enlarged military. Pakistan had lost half its territory but the size of its armed forces continued to expand. On the Indian side, euphoria over defeating Pakistan militarily bred hubris that precluded planning for a long-term peace. By 1977, Pakistan was back under direct military rule and Bhutto was executed after a show trial in 1979. The India–Pakistan relationship did not evolve as Indira Gandhi had expected, nor did Bhutto get time to prove that he could keep his end of the bargain.

The two countries had lost another opportunity to rewrite the rules of their engagement. In less than a quarter century after Independence, both sides had complicated their relationship more than they needed to. On the Pakistani side, Jinnah's optimism right after Partition had been subdued by the paranoia of Pakistan's political elites, who also had to contend with the fact that they had inherited a larger share of British India's army than its economy. In India, Mahatma Gandhi's calls for magnanimity towards Pakistan gave way to Nehru's political double-speak and Patel's aggressiveness. Kashmir became a bone of contention that strengthened the Pakistan army's role in policy-making.

After two wars, in 1965 and 1971, Pakistan lost its eastern wing but instead of tempering its ambitions for being India's equal, the loss only exacerbated anti-India sentiment. Indira Gandhi thought she had finally been magnanimous at Shimla, but Pakistanis saw the absence of pressure for a full settlement of Kashmir as an opportunity to keep conflict alive.

India still failed to convince a majority of Pakistanis that its refusal to annex Bangladesh or to carry on war against a demoralized army in West Pakistan after the fall of Dhaka represented acceptance of Pakistan as a neighbour. To start thinking of each other as neighbours rather than as adversaries would have been too rational for a relationship that has been governed by psychological factors.

2

'Kashmir Is Pakistan's Jugular Vein'

When Pakistan's Prime Minister Nawaz Sharif addressed the United Nations General Assembly in September 2015, he repeated what other Pakistani leaders have told the UN year after year. 'Since 1947, the Kashmir dispute has remained unresolved,' Sharif said, speaking emotionally of 'three generations of Kashmiris' who had 'only seen broken promises and brutal oppression'.

Sharif's statement made headlines in Pakistan, but it was hardly mentioned elsewhere in the world. Of the 193 members of the UN, Nawaz Sharif alone spoke about Kashmir. This was a far cry from earlier times. In 1948, when India originally took the issue of Jammu and Kashmir to the United Nations, complaining about armed Pakistani raiders, a majority of the UN's fifty-eight members shared Pakistan's view. The UN Security Council passed a resolution calling for a plebiscite in the state, arguing like Pakistan that the people of Jammu and Kashmir deserved self-determination. But international interest in the dispute has diminished over time. The last time the UN Security Council passed a resolution calling for plebiscite in Kashmir was in 1957, when the total UN membership was eighty-two. The reason for this and for Kashmir to remain a problem that is neither solved nor set aside lies with Pakistan, which has consistently allowed sentimentality to trump strategic thinking.

Pakistanis speak about Jammu and Kashmir emotionally as a matter of right and wrong, not in the context of realpolitik. To Pakistanis, it is the unfinished business of Partition and the 'core issue' between India and Pakistan. The Pakistani author M.M.R. Khan wrote in 1955 that 'For Pakistan, Kashmir has come to embody distrust and fear of India.' Khan argued that 'India did not accept the partition of India in good faith' and that its acceptance of Kashmir's accession reflected its intention to 'undo the division'.[1] Because Kashmir is so entwined with the idea of Pakistan, much of the Pakistani handling of the state has been unstrategic, overwrought and unsophisticated – both in the past and in the present. While India hasn't always behaved well, especially in its brutal militarization of the state and frequent human rights violations, it is Pakistan that has erred in adopting a zero-sum approach on Kashmir.

A former Pakistan army chief once remarked in a private conversation with me that after investing so much time and energy on the issue, Pakistan could not swallow the bitter pill of recognizing that the Kashmir dispute might not be resolved any time soon. Pakistanis have even ignored the advice of one of their closest friends, Chinese President Jiang Zemin, who told Pakistan's parliament in 1996, 'If certain issues cannot be resolved for the time being, they may be shelved temporarily so that they will not affect the normal state-to-state relations.'[2]

Pakistan's unstrategic thinking has led to a loss of sympathy on the issue for Pakistan among the international community and a hardening of India's position, making negotiations between the two countries next to impossible.

Pakistan has mobilized international pressure (from

1948 to 1963), waged war (in 1965), instigated armed insurrection (from 1989 to 2002), and attempted to militarily alter the Line of Control (at Kargil in 1999). It has also supported jihadi terrorism against India for years, at great cost to itself. Efforts to reignite international interest in the dispute have also continued consistently.

None of these efforts have met with real success. The 1948 ceasefire left 35 per cent of the territory of Jammu and Kashmir in Pakistan's hands and 48 per cent with India. (The rest, primarily disputed frontier land, is controlled by China.) Since then, territorial control has not changed, despite Pakistan's attempts.

At closer examination, Kashmir is not the cause of conflict between the two states but rather a symptom of it. If the rationale for Partition was to create a Muslim-majority Pakistan and a Hindu-majority India, then Pakistan cannot accept Jammu and Kashmir, with its Muslim majority, as part of India. Kashmir must be part of Pakistan to fit the contours of the two-nation theory. Equally important for India is to negate the idea of the subcontinent's division along religious lines.

The Kashmir issue might never have arisen if the

Muslim League had prepared better for Pakistani independence. The British plan for Partition freed rulers of princely states from the obligations to the British crown. Mountbatten addressed the Chamber of Princes, telling them that while they were technically independent, they should 'forge relations with the new nation closest to them'.[3] The Congress began negotiating accession with the princes right away. Nehru approached the British Viceroy well ahead of Independence Day to seek support in negotiations with them. The Muslim League, on the other hand, were completely unprepared.

Of the 562 or so princely states, only six hesitated in their accession to India. Travancore and Bhopal, one with a Hindu ruler and the other with a Muslim ruler but both with majority Hindu subjects, argued a bit before agreeing to join India. Hindu-majority Jodhpur shared a border with both India and Pakistan, and its Hindu ruler flirted with accepting Jinnah's offer to merge with Pakistan but eventually recognized that his state belonged in India. On the other hand, Junagadh's Muslim nawab ignored the fact that his tiny state was surrounded on all sides by India and had a Hindu majority. He announced accession to

Pakistan, only to be driven out of his state by the people.

Two large princely states mirrored each other in that the faith of their prince differed from the religion of the majority of their subjects. The Nizam of Hyderabad, the richest and largest princely state, thought he could maintain independence and have close ties with Pakistan against the wishes of Hyderabad's overwhelmingly Hindu population. Jammu and Kashmir's Hindu maharaja, Hari Singh, thought he too could rule his Muslim-majority population as an independent kingdom with ties with both India and Pakistan. Hari Singh signed a Standstill Agreement with Pakistan to buy time for negotiations. India refused to sign such an agreement, giving Pakistan advantage in negotiations with the maharaja.

Had the Muslim League leadership thought things through, they would have refused to accept Junagadh's accession and not even discussed accession with the maharaja of Jodhpur. Similarly, Hyderabad belonged in India under the two-nation theory, notwithstanding its Muslim ruler and the local Muslim nobility's proud traditions. Instead, Jinnah told Mountbatten that if the Congress 'attempted to exert any pressure on Hyderabad, every Muslim throughout the whole of India, yes all the hundred million Muslims, would rise as one man to defend the oldest Muslim dynasty in India'.[4] Forethought, it seems, had not been the Muslim League leadership's strong suit. They took a stand based on whatever appeared emotionally appealing at the moment, setting the stage for the showdown over Kashmir.

Ironically, the Congress leadership was divided over Kashmir, and had the Muslim League paid greater attention to princely states on the eve of Partition, Pakistan might have had less difficulty in securing Jammu and Kashmir. According to the historian Ramachandra Guha, Nehru always wanted Kashmir to be part of India but Patel was at one time inclined to allow it to join Pakistan. Patel changed his mind on 13 September 1947, the day the Pakistani government accepted the accession of Junagadh. If Pakistan could lay claim to a Hindu-majority state with a Muslim ruler, why should India not admit to its fold a Muslim-majority state with a Hindu ruler?[5]

Lacking a plan to deal with the tangled web of its relations with princely states, Pakistan sought to secure Jammu and Kashmir by fait accompli. Pakistan's armed forces were still commanded by British officers who refused to be party to coercing the maharaja of Kashmir. So Muslim League politicians, supported by senior Muslim officers of the Pakistan army, organized a tribal lashkar (militia) drawn from the areas bordering Afghanistan. The lashkar's invasion of Kashmir provided justification for the Indian army to land in Jammu and Kashmir, ostensibly after a panicked maharaja signed the Instrument of Accession on 26 October 1947. Pakistan has contested that accession ever since.

For their part, the US and the international community tried, first through the UN and later through bilateral negotiations, to help find a way out of the imbroglio. The Security Council established its Commission for India and Pakistan (UNCIP) through its resolution of 21 April 1948 and called for a plebiscite to ascertain the wishes of the Kashmiri people. The commission itself adopted a more elaborate and detailed resolution on 13 August 1948, outlining a plan for a ceasefire, a truce agreement and the proposed plebiscite. The notion of a plebiscite was reiterated in another commission resolution on 5 January

1949, followed by the Security Council's nomination of US Fleet Admiral Chester W. Nimitz as plebiscite administrator on 14 March 1950.

While Pakistan appealed to international opinion, arguing for the right of the Kashmiri people to self-determination, India was busy consolidating its control over parts of the state it had secured in the first Kashmir war, in 1948.

Nehru decided to legitimize Maharaja Hari Singh's controversial accession with the support of Kashmir's most important political leader at the time, Sheikh Abdullah, and his All Jammu and Kashmir National Conference. The Jammu and Kashmir Constituent Assembly ratified the accession in 1952, the Indian Constitution was amended to make special provision for Jammu and Kashmir, and India started asserting the state as an integral part of the nation.

Ten years later, the India–China conflict brought India closer to the United States. Soon after the 1962 war in Aksai Chin and along India's north-east border with China, the British minister for commonwealth relations, Duncan Sandys, and W. Averell Harriman, US assistant secretary of state for Far Eastern affairs, travelled to the region to propose India–Pakistan discussions on Kashmir without preconditions. Ayub turned down the idea of direct dialogue with Nehru but accepted a meeting between Cabinet-level representatives from both countries.

Harriman noted that he and Sandys had made it plain to Ayub that Pakistan's demand for a plebiscite in Kashmir could not be fulfilled and that the Vale of Kashmir, controlled by India, 'could not be transferred to Pakistan'. But the Indians understood that 'they had to make certain concessions beyond the present cease-fire line'. For his part, Ayub had already told the Americans that he was prepared to find a solution to Kashmir if three elements of the problem were taken fully into account: (1) The people of Kashmir had a stake in their future; (2) Pakistan had a stake in Kashmir; and (3) India had a stake in the area.

'Any solution reasonably satisfying these three elements would be accepted by Pakistan,' Ayub had told President Eisenhower in 1959. 'A plebiscite would be fine,' he said, but if that was not possible, he was prepared to consider any alternative which would satisfy the three points.[6]

India designated its minister for railways, Swaran Singh, a stolid, amiable Sikh politician, as its negotiator. Pakistan's representative was Zulfikar Ali Bhutto, who then served as minister for natural resources. Both men went on to become their countries' foreign ministers. During six rounds of negotiations, India offered changes in the ceasefire line that would have added 1500 square miles to Kashmir's territory controlled by Pakistan. But the Pakistani negotiators rejected the proposal because it would still leave an overwhelming Muslim population of Kashmir under Indian rule. The British and the Americans proposed third-party mediation, which India rejected.

According to one account of the 1962–63 talks, the Indian side proposed three different maps for territorial adjustments. After making the offer of an additional 1500 square miles, the Indian delegation asked the Pakistani side how they would like to modify the map. Bhutto leaned over a map and pointed to the little town of Kathua on the Kashmir–Himachal border, drew a circle somewhere there with his forefinger and said, 'You can have this part of Kashmir. We want the rest.'[7] Half a century later, Pakistan's outlook does not seem to have changed.

Undoubtedly, Pakistanis feel strongly about Kashmir. 'Kashmir is the Jugular vein of Pakistan,' Jinnah is reported to have said at the time of Partition – a quote that is committed to the memory of every schoolchild in Pakistan. More recently, General Pervez Musharraf famously declared that 'Kashmir is in our blood'. But the strong belief in the righteousness of Pakistan's claim to Kashmir has never been accompanied by a coherent strategy or a well-considered endgame to get it. Instead, its strategies were based on flawed assumptions about India, about international reactions to the Kashmir issue, and a limited understanding of history. It is Pakistan's army that has always taken the lead role in pursuing what is often described as 'the Kashmir cause'. And it is one of the many paradoxes of Pakistan that Pakistan's ability to secure international support over Kashmir declined after the army assumed direct power in 1958, even as Kashmir's centrality in Pakistan's approach to India increased.

Pakistan has fought India four times, thrice over Kashmir including the 1947–48 tribal invasion. According to Altaf Gauhar, who served as Ayub Khan's propaganda adviser, the Pakistan military has often assumed that 'the Indians are too cowardly and ill-organized to offer any effective military response which could pose a threat to Pakistan'.[8]

The belief was originally articulated by Ayub after becoming the first native commander of Pakistan's land forces in 1951. Ayub thought that, as a general rule, 'Hindu morale would not stand more than a couple of hard blows at the right time and place.'[9] Not only did this express a prejudiced, stereotyped image of Hindus, widespread in the Pakistan army, it ignored the fact that there were Sikh, Parsi, Muslim and even Jewish generals in India's multi-religious army. In 1971, the Pakistani army surrendered in Dhaka to a Sikh general, after negotiating terms with a Jew, both of whom reported to an army chief who was Parsi!

Lack of strategic thinking on Kashmir on the part of Pakistan's soldiers and military planners, together with their circumscribed knowledge of history, has also led them to assume that Muslim Kashmiris want to be part of Muslim Pakistan, and that the international community still cares about UN resolutions last passed sixty years ago. Based on those suppositions, Pakistan has rejected offers of partial solutions, hoping that the situation in Jammu and Kashmir would worsen to a point where India's grip on the state becomes untenable. Then, the international community would weigh in and force India to fulfil promises made decades ago.

Thus, Pakistan has been strong in rhetoric about Kashmir without appearing to have a well-considered plan. For example, there is no evidence that anyone in Islamabad knew what would be their second move once the Kashmir Valley was engulfed by militancy during the 1990s. Was India simply going to give in to the militants or appeal to Pakistan to let it hold a plebiscite? Similarly, the Pakistan army seemed to have no further plan after it disrupted the peace process initiated by Prime Ministers Nawaz Sharif and Atal Bihari Vajpayee, by capturing mountain peaks in Kargil in 1999.

India, on the other hand, has been more deliberate in each move on the strategic chessboard. It has made and violated promises as part of a considered blueprint. To India it is moot whether Kashmiri Muslims would have voted for Pakistan in a plebiscite sixty years ago. Whether by force or with consent, India has gradually integrated the Kashmiri population into the Indian nation. Even Kashmiri disenchantment with New Delhi cannot overcome the fact that several generations of Kashmiris since Independence have grown up with closer ties with India than with Pakistan. The Kashmiri language appears on Indian currency notes while Pakistan has only a handful of people who speak Kashmiri.

By promising, then putting off, and finally cancelling a UN-organized plebiscite in Jammu and Kashmir, India has set the stage for making it more and more difficult for Pakistan to resist absorption of Kashmir into the Indian Union. For a while, during the 1990s, Pakistan was able to take advantage of Kashmiri grievances arising from inadequate representation, erosion of the 'special status' promised to the state of Jammu and Kashmir in 1947 and the neglect of the people by their leaders. After initial involvement of Kashmiris, however, violence in the valley fell into the hands of jihadi groups recruited from among Pakistanis.

India's human rights violations and the extensive

militarization of Kashmir evoked strong international reaction that subsided once the situation improved and Pakistan's role in supporting terrorism became more visible. Pakistan's hopes of internationalizing the Kashmir dispute were dashed once again. 'Both sides are wrong,' observed the American scholar Lincoln Bloomfield in 2002. 'India for denying the population of Kashmir genuine self-determination, Pakistan for fostering terrorism, and both for blustering when prudence is called for.'[10]

Now, moral or legal arguments notwithstanding, Pakistan's position on Kashmir no longer generates much positive reaction outside Pakistan. The proliferation of Kashmir-oriented jihadi groups – such as Lashkar-e-Taiba and Jaish-e-Muhammad – and their attacks on India's civilian population have eaten away international support for Pakistan's position. Indian citizens, who were less fervent about Kashmir than Pakistanis over the years, are no longer amenable to compromise with those they see as backers and perpetrators of terrorism.

Lashkar-e-Taiba's attack on the Indian Parliament in 2001 resulted in amassing of troops by both India and Pakistan along their border. A similar response was averted in 2008, after coordinated attacks on civilians in Mumbai, killing 166 people including five Americans. According to US Secretary of State Hillary Clinton, India made it clear to her that 'there would not be such restraint in the event of a second attack'. Prime Minister Manmohan Singh and Congress chief Sonia Gandhi explained to Clinton 'how hard it had been to show restraint toward Pakistan'.[11] Give and take over Kashmir has become associated in India with making concessions to terrorists. Instead of softening India through fear, which was probably the intention of the jihadis, India's stance on negotiating with Pakistan has clearly hardened.

On the other side of the border, jihadi groups and the religious political parties that back them help maintain nationalist frenzy in Pakistan. Any Pakistani suggesting that normalization of ties with India can precede a final settlement over Kashmir runs the risk of being dubbed a 'traitor'. If discussion in Pakistan were freer than it is, there might be many takers for the idea that Pakistan normalize relations with India without insisting on resolving the Kashmir dispute first. After all, China claims sovereignty over Taiwan but is content with the status quo without pressing its claim. Like China and Taiwan, Pakistan could also work out some modus vivendi over Kashmir that does not amount to giving up its claims. Conventional wisdom in Pakistan, however, is that doing so would dilute Pakistan's ideological foundations.

In some ways, keeping Pakistani sentiment on Kashmir at a high pitch has ill served Pakistan in its ability to expand relations with India. Pakistan's Kashmir policy remains by and large in the hands of the military even when civilian prime ministers hold office. Civilian leaders who pursued alternatives to deadlocked positions found themselves weakened or out of office before being able to clinch the deal, as did Musharraf, a military ruler.

When Indian Prime Minister Manmohan Singh spoke in 2006 of a 'treaty of peace, security and friendship' with Pakistan, he inadvertently highlighted the different visions of India–Pakistan relations prevailing in Delhi and Islamabad. India sees normalization as a means of addressing disputes and issues that have proved intractable over more than six decades. Pakistan, on the other hand, continues to insist that normalization would be the end result, rather than the means, of resolving disputes, especially the Kashmir question. The experience of other countries embroiled in similar disputes indicates that the 'friendship first' approach works more effectively than 'settlement first'.

Perhaps demanding a resolution of the Kashmir issue before opening up trade or travel is the Pakistani establishment's way of ensuring that India and Pakistan remain apart. That is why Pakistan responded to Manmohan Singh's offer by saying that it would be 'unrealistic' to expect Pakistan to move forward without progress on the Kashmir issue and its foreign ministry reiterated that the status quo – meaning the Line of Control – was not acceptable to Pakistanis or Kashmiris.

That exchange, with India calling for normalization and Pakistan insisting on 'resolving' Kashmir first without offering alternative intermediate solutions, encapsulates the predicament of India–Pakistan discussions. Negotiations usually involve reconciling maximum demands – what one side says it desires – with its minimal expectation, what it will settle for. Most observers agree that India's maximum demand is that Pakistan give up its claim on all of Jammu and Kashmir, and its minimal expectation would probably be that Pakistan accept the status quo without further violence, and a de facto partition of Kashmir along the Line of Control.

An Indian negotiating team would try to secure more than the minimum and would probably settle for less than the maximum. In recent public pronouncements, Indian leaders have made more or less official their preference for settling the Kashmir issue on the basis of legitimizing the status quo, with territorial adjustments similar to the ones offered in 1963. In Pakistan, however, there has never been much discussion of a 'bottom line' national position on the Kashmir conflict. When Musharraf repeatedly offered a four-point prescription between 2003 and 2006 to resolve the Kashmir issue, his formulation was uncannily similar to that of Ayub in his conversation with Eisenhower in 1959.

Ayub had enunciated the need for the deal to reflect the interests of Kashmiris, Pakistan and India. Musharraf spoke of fashioning the compromise 'through a process of elimination' to 'eliminate anything not acceptable to India, Pakistan, and the Kashmiris'.[12] It is significant that between 1959 and 2006, neither Pakistan nor India has substantially altered its bargaining positions. Through the process of elimination, it is clear that what is unacceptable to Pakistan is the status quo, the de facto division of the erstwhile princely state of Jammu and Kashmir that leaves India in control of the Muslim-majority Kashmir Valley. India, on the other hand, is willing to offer territorial compromises without tacitly accepting the two-nation theory by ceding all of Kashmir.

Normalization of relations with India, an emerging global power that is also the strategic partner of the world's sole superpower, is far more important for Pakistan today than it was in the early years of its life as an independent state. The problem for Pakistan's ruling elite is that after sixty-nine years of describing Kashmir as Pakistan's primary national 'cause' it is not easy, especially for an overbearing military, to effectively manage a major shift in national priorities.

In June 1972 Sidney Sober, then acting ambassador of the United States to Pakistan, had observed that instead of becoming more pragmatic, Pakistanis had started embracing the cause of Kashmiri self-determination a little more vehemently after the loss of Bangladesh.[13] His concerns matched those of US Secretary of State Dean Rusk, who had complained after the failure of the 1963 Bhutto–Swaran Singh talks that 'nothing less than a Franco-German type of reconciliation is likely to work' between India and Pakistan. France and Germany are now pillars of an integrated Europe after seventy-five years of conflict, including two world wars.

'India is more ready for this than Pakistan,' Rusk had noted, adding that Pakistan 'appears most reluctant to ease pressures on Kashmir by discussing or agreeing on other questions prior to a Kashmir settlement'. Observing that 'Pakistan pretends to be convinced that India has never accepted partition and seeks the disappearance of Pakistan',[14] he realized that a Kashmir settlement was not possible without a fundamental change in the mindset of the Pakistani establishment.

Pakistan assumed that Kashmir would become part of Pakistan by the logic of Partition. It did not prepare to secure the state's accession and tried to make up for that error through use of force. The invasion of Kashmir by tribal raiders played into India's hands, giving India the pretext to incorporate the state. Since then, India has strategically made and broken promises with Kashmiris about self-determination and special status. It managed to ride through UN demands for a plebiscite with a series of similar premeditated steps. Pakistan still lacks an endgame for Kashmir, acting emotionally and reacting to India's deliberate actions with military incursions, terrorism and appeals for international support that increasingly fall on deaf ears.

Instead of setting aside the dispute for the moment to normalize relations with India, Pakistan's military insists on resolution of the Kashmir imbroglio before opening trade or travel. The absence of a Pakistani strategy for final success leaves little hope for Pakistan getting its way on Kashmir. The insistence on resolving this issue before all others only means that Kashmir holds back normalization between India and Pakistan. The two neighbours are now nuclear weapons powers, making it impossible for them to fight wars like the ones in 1948, 1965 and 1971.

Is Kashmir really Pakistan's 'jugular vein' if the country has survived for sixty-nine years without it? If it is not critical for the survival of either India or Pakistan, should the two risk nuclear mass destruction over a quarrel they have not been able to resolve for so long?

3

'We Should Use the Nuclear Bomb'

An American journalist travelling through Pakistan in 2002 was taken aback at the sight of the 'craggy, Gibraltarish replica of a nameless peak in the Chagai range in the center of the biggest traffic circle of every major city'. That craggy peak in Balochistan was Pakistan's nuclear test site. The journalist, Peter Landesman, went on to observe: 'The development, in 1998, of the "Islamic Bomb," intended as a counter to India's nuclear capability, is Pakistan's only celebrated achievement since its formation, in 1947.' That harsh comment paled before his account of a conversation with a retired, 'slightly depressed' Pakistani brigadier in his early fifties, who had once served as head of Pakistan's military intelligence in Sindh Province.

Landesman and Brigadier Amanullah had met at the Islamabad house of former prime minister Benazir Bhutto, for whom Amanullah worked after retiring from the army. There, a painting caught Landesman's eye. It depicted Pakistan's founder, Jinnah, as a towering figure, flanked by other leaders, with Islamabad spread out below them. 'Jinnah's arm pointed to the vast plain beyond the city, where a rocket was lifting out of billowing clouds of vapor and fire into the sky,' Landesman recalled. The brigadier noticed the journalist looking at the painting and the two spoke about what it represented. 'A nuclear warhead heading to India,' said the brigadier. Landesman initially thought the retired soldier was making a joke, and then realized that he wasn't.

The American expressed his consternation over 'the ease with which Pakistanis talk of nuclear war with India'. 'No,' the brigadier responded matter-of-factly: 'This should happen. We should use the bomb.' In the brigadier's opinion, it was all right for Pakistan to use nukes not only in retaliation but also for a first strike.

The brigadier then 'launched into a monologue' that reflected both his anger and his depression. 'We should fire at them and take out a few of their cities – Delhi, Bombay, Calcutta,' he said. 'They should fire back and take Karachi and Lahore. Kill off a hundred or two hundred million people.... They have acted so badly toward us; they have been so mean. We should teach them a lesson. It would teach all of us a lesson.'

The brigadier's monologue continued: 'There is no future here, and we need to start over.... So many people think this. Have you been to the villages of Pakistan, the interior? There is nothing but dire poverty and pain. The children have no education; there is nothing to look forward to. Go into the villages, see the poverty. There is no drinking water. Small children without shoes walk miles for a drink of water. I go to the villages and I want to cry. My children have no future. None of the children of Pakistan have a future. We are surrounded by nothing but war and suffering. Millions should die away.'

The brigadier blamed India squarely for Pakistan's backwardness, not its leaders' decisions to invest in the military at the expense of human development. And he seemed to ignore completely the extent of India's own poverty. To him, a nuclear attack was justified because

'Tens of thousands of people are dying in Kashmir, and the only superpower says nothing.' He complained that America had sided with India because it has interests there and repeated that he was willing to see his children be killed.[1]

Of course, Landesman's account, which he published under the title 'A Modest Proposal from the Brigadier', does not represent policy or even reasoned discussion in Pakistan's decision-making circles. It does, however, reflect the fervour that has led Pakistan to become the world's only nuclear weapon power (excluding possibly North Korea) that abjures committing to a 'no first use' policy about weapons of mass destruction. Pakistan is also the only country in the world that publicly says that its nukes exist solely for defence against a specific country – India.

As recently as March 2016, Pakistan's foreign affairs adviser, Sartaj Aziz, said that 'India, not terrorism, is the biggest threat to the region' and asked India to reduce its nuclear stockpile so that Pakistan can consider reciprocation. The claim of India being the biggest threat seemed hollow, given that 40,000 Pakistanis have reportedly been killed or injured at the hands of terrorists.

Pakistan's economy, its international relations and the ability of its citizens to travel abroad with ease have all suffered because of it. Still Sartaj Aziz insisted that India imperiled Pakistan more than terrorism. He reflects Pakistan's fixation with India, which US President George W. Bush once described as an 'obsession'.

Aziz said that Pakistan's nuclear arsenal was a major deterrent against India, and 'If they increase the stockpile, we cannot reduce ours.'[2] This stance – that one country's nuclear posture is tied solely to that of another – differs from that of all other major nuclear-armed powers. When the United States first developed nuclear weapons, and the Soviet Union, Britain, France and China followed suit, they did so on the grounds of pursuing a global security role. The US dropped atomic bombs on Japan to end the Second World War long before it was concerned about the Soviet Union.

India's nuclear programme also originated not out of a regional rivalry, but from the argument that non-proliferation should be global. Either no one should have weapons of mass destruction or everyone has the right to have them. Pakistan's nuclear programme, on the other hand, is about contention with India. Pakistan developed, and continues to develop, nuclear bombs as a direct response to India, nothing more and nothing else.

Initially, India was a strong advocate of global elimination of nuclear weapons. Under Nehru, nuclear energy for civilian purposes was declared desirable but nuclear weapons were not. Still, India did not give up on a nuclear weapons option, to make the point about the equal right of all nations to do what the superpowers did. Defeat in the Sino-Indian war of 1962 and the Chinese nuclear test of 1964 led to a drastic change in India's direction. India refused to sign the Nuclear Non-Proliferation Treaty (NPT), as did Pakistan, and work started on India's nuclear weapons. In 1974 India conducted its first nuclear tests. Unlike India, Pakistan did not relate its refusal to adhere to the NPT to the prospect of global nuclear apartheid. Pakistan's position was, and remains to this day, that its nuclear posture will be based on responding to 'the Indian threat'. For years, Pakistani officials declared that Pakistan would join the nuclear restraint regimes the day India does the same.

Moreover, contrary to a widely held belief, Pakistan did

not start working on building nuclear weapons only after India's 1974 tests. Bhutto reportedly assembled nuclear scientists at Multan in January 1972, not even one month after Pakistan's humiliating military defeat in Bangladesh, and called upon them to chart a quick path to nuclear weapons status. 'We will eat grass,' Bhutto famously remarked about Pakistan having an atomic bomb, 'but we will get one of our own. We have no other choice.' Pursuit of the bomb, then, was about restoring Pakistan's wounded pride and preventing military humiliation like the one at Dhaka, and not just about keeping up with a nuclear India.

Feroz Hassan Khan, who served in the Pakistan army's nuclear Strategic Plans Division, has written the definitive book on how and why Pakistan made the bomb. The book is aptly titled *Eating Grass: The Making of the Pakistani Bomb*. 'Pakistani senior officials tapped into the genius of young scientists and engineers and molded them into a motivated cadre of weaponeers,' he wrote proudly, adding that nuclear developments were interwoven with 'the broad narrative of Pakistani nationalism'. Thus, Pakistan's nukes have 'evolved into the most significant symbol of national determination and a central element of Pakistan's identity'. They reflect 'Pakistan's enduring rivalry and strategic competition with India'.[3]

Unlike scientists in most countries, who avoid politics, several Pakistani nuclear scientists became active proponents of Islamist and anti-Indian state ideology. The most prominent among them was Dr Abdul Qadeer Khan, a metallurgist who advanced Pakistan's nuclear weapons programme by bringing with him (some would say stealing) designs and specifications from the Dutch uranium enrichment plant where he worked in the early 1970s. A.Q. Khan, as he became known, also headed the procurement network that enabled Pakistan to covertly acquire equipment for its nuclear facilities from all over the world. After helping build Pakistan's bomb, A.Q. Khan went on to sell the designs and material for nukes to Libya, Iran and North Korea, claiming in a 2004 televised confession that he did so only for personal financial gain and not as Pakistani state policy. That somewhat implausible claim helped protect Pakistan from international sanctions for nuclear proliferation to regimes considered dangerous by most of the world.

A.Q. Khan had an exaggerated sense of self and loved publicity. I met him in 1996 in my capacity as adviser to Prime Minister Benazir Bhutto at a time A.Q. Khan wanted Pakistan's highest civilian award, Nishan-e-Pakistan, which he was awarded that August. He told me that Pakistanis had not honoured him enough, given the fact that he had ensured Pakistan's survival forever. In any other country, A.Q. Khan felt, he would have been elevated to the presidency for life in addition to being considered the country's protecting angel. He lit up whenever someone referred to him as 'Mohsin-e-Pakistan' (Benefactor of Pakistan) and wondered why that title could not be conferred on him formally by Pakistan's parliament.

In his many interviews and sponsored biographies, A.Q. Khan told the story of how he reacted to Pakistan's defeat in the 1971 war, met Zulfikar Ali Bhutto and offered to share technology he was working on in the Netherlands that would help Pakistan become a nuclear weapons power. Fear and hatred for India was his sole motivation though later he became vehemently anti-American, too, because of US opposition to Pakistan's nuclear ambitions.

A.Q. Khan wrote in 2011, 'For a country that couldn't produce bicycle chains to have become a nuclear and missile power within a short span – and in the teeth of Western opposition – was quite a feat.' According to him, Pakistan achieved nuclear capacity by the second half of the 1980s while it perfected the delivery system by the early 1990s. This had been possible only because 'I wanted to save my country from Indian nuclear blackmail'.[4] In an interview soon after Pakistan's nuclear tests in 1998, he spoke bitterly of his family's migration from Bhopal, where he was born, saying that 'All the way from Bhopal to the borders of Pakistan, the Hindus were very cruel.'

He argued that Pakistanis and Indians were basically different because, 'We are Muslims, they are Hindus. We eat cows. They worship cows. That we lived on the same land and spoke the same language does not make us the same people.'[5] A letter by A.Q. Khan in 1980 while responding to a report about him in the British newspaper *Observer* provides insight into his mind. 'Shyam Bhatia, a Hindu bastard, could not write anything objective about Pakistan,' he wrote, referring to the author of the article.[6]

A.Q. Khan was not alone among Pakistan's nuclear

scientists in being motivated by a hardline anti-India ideology. Another important figure in Pakistan's nuclear missile programme, Dr Samar Mubarakmand, publicly boasted of Pakistan's ability to 'wipe out entire India from the subcontinent in few seconds'.[7] Contrary to Pakistan's focus on India in pursuit of its nuclear weapons programme, India rationalized its nukes as a step on the ladder to global great power status.

Pakistan's scientists were assisted by soldiers and civilians alike in their effort to create a deterrent to India. Businessmen and even smugglers offered their services to the state to help put together everything needed to enrich uranium and produce atomic bombs. Jamsheed Marker, a prominent Parsi who served for three decades as ambassador in Ghana, Japan, the Soviet Union, Germany, France and the United States, wrote in his memoirs about cloak-and-dagger operations through Pakistani embassies that helped build Pakistan's nuclear arsenal.

'This exercise involved a bit of James Bond stuff,' he explained, describing the role of embassy officers from a special Procurement Directorate whose sole purpose was to clandestinely buy items required by A.Q. Khan and his team, most of which were restricted by the laws of various countries. Marker describes his meetings as ambassador to Germany with 'characters, genuine and shady, in tiny cafes tucked away in obscure villages deep in the beautiful Swiss and German countryside'. According to Marker, western industrial enterprises conspired with Pakistan 'to evade their own governments' law prohibiting all nuclear transfers to Pakistan' in pursuit of profit.[8]

For Pakistanis, deception and violation of other countries' laws in the process of becoming India's equal in nuclear technology is a matter of pride, as attested by the willingness of a diplomat of Marker's international standing to publicly reveal the subterfuge. India most likely broke rules in assembling material for its nuclear weapons, too, but its scientists and diplomats have avoided bragging.

According to Feroz Khan, three important beliefs define Pakistani strategic thinking. First, 'nuclear weapons are the only guarantee of Pakistan's national survival in the face of both an inverterately hostile India that cannot be deterred conventionally and unreliable external allies that fail to deliver in extremis. Second, Pakistan's nuclear program is unfairly singled out for international opposition because of its Muslim population. This feeling of victimization is accentuated by a belief that India consistently "gets away with" violating global non-proliferation norms. Third is the belief that India, Israel or the United States might use military force to stop Pakistan's nuclear program.' These beliefs have only strengthened 'the determination of Pakistan's military, bureaucratic, and scientific establishment to pay any political, economic or technical cost to reach their objective of a nuclear armed Pakistan'.[9]

While Pakistan's nukes are centred on India, India's prime minister, Atal Bihari Vajpayee, did not even mention Pakistan when India made public its status as a nuclear weapons power with five test detonations on 11 May and 13 May 1998. Vajpayee's address to parliament focused on India's right to possess nuclear weapons in a world that still had such weapons. In a letter to US President Bill Clinton, Vajpayee spoke only of China as the major threat to India and that was to secure US support, given US concerns about potential long-term rivalry with China in the Indo-Pacific region. But in Pakistan, the Indian tests were interpreted as a direct threat. Pakistan conducted its own tests in underground tunnels below the Chagai mountains two tense weeks later.

Since India's tests involved five detonations, the number of Pakistani explosions had to be six, one more than the Indians. Pakistanis celebrated what they perceived to be parity or even superiority to India. The *Washington Post* summed up the euphoria in Islamabad in the words, 'We have done it. We are India's equal.'[10] Fiberglass replicas of the Chagai mountains, and also of missiles named after Muslim invaders of India, were installed at major intersections in all major cities shortly thereafter.

US sanctions, imposed on both India and Pakistan after their nuclear tests, hit Pakistan's economy harder, given the country's more precarious foreign currency reserves. Private foreign currency accounts, previously guaranteed by the government, were frozen and account holders received their savings in Pakistani rupees. Across-the-board cuts were imposed on public spending, and development projects were suspended. The nation's resolve to 'eat grass' for nuclear status appeared on the verge of being put to test.

But after a while, the American tendency to stop examining the past and look for ways to move forward kicked in. First, the International Monetary Fund came to Pakistan's rescue and later American sanctions mellowed as Washington decided to engage India and Pakistan instead of punishing them. Clinton and his foreign policy team encouraged the South Asian neighbours to mend the ways in which they saw each other, now that they both had weapons of mass destruction.

Rationalists in India also argued that a Nixon-to-China moment had arrived, when India and Pakistan could finally end their enmity. If only the Hindu nationalist prime minister Vajpayee would travel to Pakistan and talk to the Muslim nationalist Pakistani leader Nawaz Sharif, they argued, middle ground between the two countries could be found. After all, the US and the Soviet Union had managed hostilities at the height of the Cold War better under the spectre of mutually assured destruction.

Vajpayee did indeed travel to Lahore in February 1999 and attempted to reassure Pakistanis of India's acceptance of their country, and to express the desire for friendship. He visited Minar-e-Pakistan, the memorial marking the site where the demand for Pakistan was first made in 1940. There he signed the Visitor's Book with a much publicized statement: 'India and Indians have accepted the creation of Pakistan and wish it well.' He emphatically declared that India harboured no reservations about Partition and accepted Pakistan's creation and right to exist as an independent state.

Vajpayee and Sharif jointly signed the 'Lahore Declaration', eschewing violence, reiterating the Simla Accord of 1972, and committing both sides to a multi-track diplomatic process that has since been variously labelled 'confidence building measures', 'comprehensive dialogue' or 'composite dialogue'. Hopes were raised that the two newly declared nuclear weapon states of South Asia, confident that one of them could no longer militarily threaten the other without risking annihilation, would now start interacting more normally.

Like all stories in the Indian subcontinent, things did not proceed as predicted. Within a few months, a new twist had appeared in the India–Pakistan saga.

Undeterred by his prime minister's commitment to normal ties with India, Pakistan's army chief General

Pervez Musharraf decided to plot and execute what he considered a brilliant plan to force India's hand on the question of Jammu and Kashmir. Musharraf had trained as a commando and often thought like one. Commandos are taught to focus on their mission, surprise the enemy and shoot from the hip. They are by training more tactical than strategic. Many years later, George W. Bush observed that Musharraf sounded reasonable until the subject of India came up, at which point his visceral dislike and mistrust of India came through.

In Kargil in 1999, Pakistani troops crossed the Line of Control to take over Indian positions vacated during winter. Musharraf and some of his generals assumed that their control of heights overlooking a key arterial highway would force India to reopen negotiations on the status of the disputed state. Benazir Bhutto told me that in 1995, when Musharraf was director-general military operations, he had proposed a similar manoeuvre to her but, as prime minister, she had overruled the idea, asking Musharraf to consider the political consequences of his plan. Whether Sharif mistakenly signed off on the venture or was never fully informed of its scope is still debated. The sequence of what followed is not.

After Pakistan's initial success, India counterattacked, inflicting heavy losses on the Pakistani troops. Musharraf had expected India to submit to an alteration of the Line of Control without a fight. He also did not anticipate India's use of air power. Instead of uniting the international community behind efforts for a final settlement over Kashmir, the ensuing war only attracted calls for Pakistan to go back to its original positions.

For Vajpayee (and Indians in general), the war in Kargil was a great betrayal. It violated the spirit of the concord the Indian prime minister had thrashed out with Pakistan's civilian leaders in Lahore. Kargil also affirmed that the Pakistani military had not changed its visceral hostility towards India, and that the traditional concept of nuclear deterrence, understood to be a disincentive for all violence between nuclear powers, would not work between India and Pakistan.

For most countries, nuclear weapons are the ultimate guarantee against being crushed by a more powerful non-nuclear force. If Pakistan's real concern had been what its officials had argued for years – that India would some day attack it and so it needed to defend itself against that attack –acquisition of nuclear weapons should have been enough to end that fear. Instead, Pakistan's generals were still looking for something they could describe to their people as a 'victory over India'. They seemed determined to try to change the territorial status quo in Kashmir by force, which was unacceptable not only to India but also to Pakistan's major international backers, the United States and China, and also to the rest of the world.

The world has never known a nuclear-armed country to recklessly initiate war with another nuclear-armed state. In that sense, Kargil broke new ground in the strategic conceptualization of nuclear deterrence. Nukes have usually helped maintain the status quo as neither side wants extermination while trying to eliminate the other. Musharraf, however, had gambled that he could change ground realities with conventional military action, and that India would bow down out of fear of escalation to nuclear conflict. He lost. As with other military adventures initiated by Pakistan's politician-generals, the Kargil war ended with the intervention of the great powers. Indian and Pakistani forces returned to their pre-war positions and the border – or Line of Control – remained where it has been since 1948.

While the Kargil episode had no long-term impact on the territory controlled by each side in Jammu and Kashmir, it intensified Indian mistrust of Pakistan, especially the Pakistan army. The official committee set up to examine India's failings in the wake of Kargil concluded that Pakistan had been 'able to commit limited aggression in Kashmir' because India had neglected the threat from Pakistan. According to the committee, Pakistan had obtained 'a proven design' for a nuclear weapon from China as far back as 1983 and had openly or implicitly threatened India with nukes at several occasions, beginning in 1987. Effective nuclear deterrence was likely to have been in place between India and Pakistan since at least 1990. It was out of fear of escalation to the nuclear level that India did not use its larger non-nuclear military force in the nine years preceding both countries' 1998 nuclear tests despite complaining about proxy war by Pakistan in Kashmir.[11]

India's civil–military compartmentalization was also blamed for not dealing more effectively with the risk of Pakistan's piecemeal attacks after acquiring atomic bombs. Apparently, the Indian military was kept 'in the dark about India's nuclear capability' whereas Pakistan's military 'as the custodian of Pakistani nuclear weaponry was fully aware of its own capability'.

Indian prime ministers, even while supporting the nuclear weapons programme, kept their intelligence and nuclear weapons establishments in two watertight compartments. 'This secretiveness on the part of the Indian Prime Ministers and the country's inability to exercise its conventional superiority,' asserted the Kargil Committee, encouraged Pakistan to 'pursue the proxy war and the Kargil adventure with impunity on the basis of its own prescribed rules of the game'. Implicit in the Kargil Committee's review was the suggestion that India had encouraged Pakistan to be more aggressive by acting as if Pakistan did not matter or was a lesser threat, and that during Kargil Pakistan had failed to create a real nuclear flashpoint only because India did not cross the Line of Control.

Kargil brought into question Pakistan's position as a responsible nuclear nation but the problem posed by the kind of conduct demonstrated by Musharraf and his team during Kargil is far from over. International opinion alone cannot overcome the threat of nuclear weapons in the subcontinent. China continues to support Pakistan to maintain a balance of power in the subcontinent though, since Kargil, Chinese leaders have been more open in encouraging Pakistan to temper its anti-Indian adventurism. The United States has made security of Pakistan's nuclear weapons and containment of its ambitions regarding weapons of mass destruction a greater priority.

Americans believe that their intervention prevented the Kargil crisis from expanding into a nuclear Armageddon. 'President Clinton engaged in one of the most sensitive diplomatic high wire acts of any administration,' says the former CIA analyst Bruce Riedel, giving credit to the US president for 'successfully persuading Pakistani Prime Minister Nawaz Sharif to pull back Pakistani-backed fighters from a confrontation with India that could threaten to escalate into a nuclear war between the world's two newest nuclear powers'.

Riedel was one of three persons in the room when

Clinton faced Sharif in 1999 in an unusual Washington DC meeting on the fourth of July, American Independence Day. The US had 'disturbing information about Pakistan preparing its nuclear arsenal for possible use'. Sharif was 'distraught, deeply worried about the direction the crisis was going toward disaster, but equally worried about his own hold on power and the threat from his military chiefs who were pressing for a tough stand'.

Although Sharif had originally been groomed for politics in the 1980s by President Zia-ul-Haq and Lt Gen. Ghulam Jilani Khan, former chief of the Inter-Services Intelligence Directorate (ISI), he had become his own man after becoming prime minister for the first time in 1991. As a Punjabi businessman, Sharif now reflected the interests and aspirations of urban Punjabis. Sharif and his Punjabi voters embrace traditional Pakistani nationalism, along with its Islamic elements, but no longer wanted the army to dictate policies. This, coupled with his deference to the United States and his desire for better relations with India, made Sharif wary of the army that had originally launched his political career.

According to Riedel's account, Clinton reportedly

framed the day's discussion by handing Sharif a cartoon from the *Chicago Tribune* newspaper that showed Pakistan and India as nuclear bombs fighting with each other. Sharif then went into 'a long and predictable defense of the Kashmiri cause' and appealed to Clinton 'to intervene directly to settle the dispute by pressing India'. But Clinton would have none of that argument. He pushed back by reminding Sharif that the US played a role in the Arab-Israeli conflict because both sides invited it to mediate, which is not the case with Kashmir. 'The best approach was the road begun at Lahore, that is direct contact with India,' he said, adding, 'Pakistan had completely undermined that opening by attacking at Kargil; it must now retreat before disaster set in.'

The more Sharif tried to bring the discussion to Kashmir, the more Clinton insisted that the fundamental reality of the day was that the Pakistani army and its militant allies were on the wrong side of the LOC and must withdraw. Clinton warned, notes Riedel, that there could be no quid pro quo and no hint that America was rewarding Pakistan for its aggression, nor for threatening to aim its nuclear arsenal at India.

At one point Clinton threatened that 'he had a draft statement ready to issue that would pin all the blame for the Kargil crisis on Pakistan tonight'. He spoke in an angry tone. 'Did Sharif order the Pakistani nuclear missile force to prepare for action? Did he realize how crazy that was?' Riedel recounted Clinton as asking.

At the end of the fateful meeting, Sharif announced withdrawal of Pakistani forces from Kargil, acknowledging the sanctity of the Line of Control. He was removed from power by Musharraf in a coup d'état a few months later. The longer-term consequence of Kargil was loss of Indian enthusiasm for a post-nuclear-test normalization with Pakistan. Delhi would no longer trust Islamabad as much as Vajpayee had trusted Nawaz Sharif. Moreover, the Americans had become convinced that Pakistan was more reckless than India with nuclear weapons.

Riedel argues correctly that the Kargil crisis 'accelerated the road to a fundamental reconciliation between the world's two largest democracies, India and the United States'.[12] In his view, the India–America entente could, over time, force Pakistan to reconsider its options in relation to India provided India does not lapse into intransigence towards the US.

For his part, Clinton began a process of isolating and pressuring Musharraf – a process that could not continue after Al-Qaeda's attacks in New York and Washington on 11 September 2001. Initially bereft of US support, Musharraf began his tenure as military dictator with an acceleration of jihadi terrorism in Jammu and Kashmir and its extension beyond the Himalayan state into the rest of India. The jihadis had a base in Taliban-controlled Afghanistan and were operating against India from Nepal and Bangladesh. For example, they were able to hijack an Indian Airlines flight from Nepal to Kandahar to secure the release of three prominent Kashmiri militants from Indian prisons. The 9/11 attacks resulted in enormous pressure on Musharraf to break ties with the Taliban regime in Afghanistan and support the US-led coalition against global terrorism. Musharraf partly obliged by helping the Americans in arresting some Al-Qaeda leaders but continued covert support for the Afghan Taliban and the anti-India terrorist groups.

After another threat of war in 2002, this time over the terrorist attack on the Indian parliament, the United

States facilitated India and Pakistan to start a dialogue again. Musharraf kept talks with India going under the shadow of both nuclear weapons and terrorism, still pushing his theory that limited war could be sustained effectively because the presence of nukes made escalation too dangerous and, therefore, unlikely.

During his nine-year stint as military dictator, Musharraf's emissaries allegedly worked out an elaborate deal with the Indian negotiator Satinder Lambah, including a final settlement on Kashmir, in protracted back-channel negotiations. But the sincerity and effectiveness of that process came into question when details of that 'near deal' could not be found in Pakistan's foreign office after Musharraf lost power in 2008. I arrived at the Pakistan foreign office, after being designated ambassador-at-large by Prime Minister Yusuf Raza Gilani soon after his election, to be told by Foreign Secretary Riaz Muhammad Khan that he, and others in the foreign ministry, had no record of the back-channel negotiations. He referred me to army chief General Ashfaq Kayani, who had previously headed the ISI, only to be told that it might be best for negotiations to start afresh. If a deal had indeed been agreed to by Musharraf, the Pakistani military clearly was not prepared to let that deal go through.

After Musharraf's departure from the presidency in 2008, the elected government went on to complete its term, the first time that had happened in Pakistan's history. However, civilian authority did not extend to major foreign policy initiatives, which remained effectively subject to a military veto. The civilian president Asif Zardari's vision of regional integration, including his professed willingness to abjure first use of nuclear weapons, was blown to pieces by Lashkar-e-Taiba's terrorist attack in Mumbai on 26 November 2008 within a couple of months of Zardari's election.

Hopes of dialogue have been renewed again after the return to office in Pakistan of Nawaz Sharif in 2013 and more so since the election of Narendra Modi as prime minister of India in 2014. Still, the two sides have seldom discussed nuclear matters. The only agreement they have ever reached in this field is the 1989 agreement signed by Rajiv Gandhi and Benazir Bhutto providing for an annual exchange of lists of nuclear installations in each country.

In recent years, Pakistan has started work on a plan

to build low-yield 'tactical' nuclear weapons that can be deployed in the battlefield. Pakistani generals say it is a response to an offensive Indian military doctrine, the Cold Start Doctrine, which India says is not a new doctrine but an operational concept for redeployment of regular forces along the border for swifter action.

Lt Gen. Khalid Kidwai, who served for several years as head of the Strategic Plans Division, listed circumstances in which Pakistan would respond to a conventional attack with nuclear weapons: 'India attacks Pakistan and conquers a large part of its territory; India destroys a large part of Pakistan's land or air forces; India blockades Pakistan in an effort to strangle it economically; or India pushes Pakistan into a state of political destabilization or creates large- scale internal subversion in the country.'[13] 'Cold Start' apparently is the Indian concept of 'developing the ability to respond to a Pakistani proxy war with conventional force while remaining below the nuclear threshold'.

In a 2009 diplomatic cable leaked on WikiLeaks, then US ambassador to India Timothy Roemer said that the Cold Start Doctrine has never been and may never be put to use on a battlefield because of substantial and serious resource constraints. He described it as 'a developed operational attack plan announced in 2004 and intended to be taken off the shelf and implemented within a 72-hour period during a crisis'.

According to Roemer, Cold Start is not a plan for a comprehensive invasion and occupation of Pakistan; 'Instead, it calls for a rapid, time- and distance-limited penetration into Pakistani territory with the goal of quickly punishing Pakistan, possibly in response to a Pakistan-linked terrorist attack in India, without threatening the survival of the Pakistani state or provoking a nuclear response.'[14]

Pakistan's military, however, already upset over the US–India civil nuclear deal, has cited Cold Start as the basis for expanding its nuclear arsenal and putting it in the hands of battlefield commanders. The decision to deploy 'strategic weapons', launched through missiles and planes, is usually controlled by generals and political leaders whom one expects to look at the bigger picture. Low-yield 'tactical nukes', on the other hand, are in the hands of field commanders and junior officers. Introducing these in the South Asian theatre of war would disperse decision-making about killing thousands of people in the hands of people like the brigadier who ruminated with the American journalist Landesman about letting millions of people die as a way out of South Asia's misery.

Pakistani generals do not always see nuclear weapons as a threat to humanity. For them it is more important that India and Pakistan be considered as peers. Pakistan insists that it must get from the Americans what India got (in this case, a civil nuclear deal). If it does not, Pakistan will level the field in a way of its own choosing. It would make more nuclear weapons and let its colonels and brigadiers decide when to use them. That neither India nor Pakistan is ready for a nuclear war – for example, neither has ever built nuclear shelters for its people – is considered irrelevant. India, single-minded in its quest for global power status, has never been willing to discuss, let alone make, any concession on nuclear issues that could help dampen the nuclear competition on the subcontinent.

So far there have been no international takers for Pakistan's latest effort to be seen on a par with India in the nuclear realm. President George W. Bush had brushed aside the possibility of a Pakistani-American civil nuclear deal to equalize the two neighbours after the India–US arrangement. He had pointed to the 'very different histories' in the nuclear field of the two nations, a reference to the nuclear arms bazaar run by the Pakistani nuclear scientist A.Q. Khan as well as Pakistan's role in the Kargil war and its continued support to terrorism.

The Pakistani physicist and social activist Pervez Hoodbhoy has often argued that having more nuclear warheads is not a matter of pride. He wrote in an article that Pakistan already has around 120 Hiroshima-sized warheads, which could increase to around 350. This would exceed numbers held by France (290), China (240) and UK (190). 'What is the number that Pakistan "must have"?' asked Hoodbhoy, adding that seventy years ago just one bomb had turned Hiroshima to rubble.

Hoodbhoy bemoaned the fact that if Pakistan and India used even half their arsenals, 'the radioactive ash and smoke would destroy not just both countries but also cause a global environmental catastrophe'. Nevertheless, neither specifies a cap. 'Deterrence is purely psychological,' he pointed out, and nobody on the subcontinent has a clue about what is sufficient. Hoodbhoy recalled his arguments during the 1980s and 1990s with the Indian strategist K. Subrahmanyam, who had asserted that 'nuclear arms racing was a Cold War concept totally alien to subcontinental thinking'. It had been assumed erroneously that the much wiser South Asians would limit destruction only to 'what was needed'.

But then, for years Subrahmanyam had also believed that Pakistan could not develop nuclear weapons. India may have only wanted to deter China or prove a point against dividing the world between nuclear haves and have-nots. It is now also stuck in an arms race with Pakistan, amid all the pathologies of bitterness handed down since Partition. 'India and Pakistan are seeing the emergence of a nuclear military-industrial complex that is distorting priorities,' says Hoodbhoy.[15] He reminds everyone that if we have a nuclear war, both India and Pakistan will win, but at the end of it neither will exist.

Pakistan built nuclear weapons in its uncompromising quest for parity with India and in response to its fear psychosis about India wanting to undo Partition. Although Pakistanis feel great pride in their having achieved nuclear power status, nuclear weapons have neither made Pakistan more secure nor created the equivalence with India that Pakistan seeks. For its part, India has done little to reassure Pakistanis and to take away the justification for a nuclear arms race. India, intent on seeing itself in global rather than regional terms, seems willing to ignore the dangers inherent in possession of nuclear weapons by two bitter neighbours. The situation is complicated further by terrorism in the subcontinent, which adds a dimension unknown to the world since the advent of nuclear weapons. Never before have nuclear-armed nations faced provocation by terrorism on their own soil.

4

Terrorism = Irregular Warfare

In March 2016, Pakistan's national security adviser, Lt Gen. (Retd) Naseer Khan Janjua, shared intelligence with his Indian counterpart, Ajit Doval, about a plot by Pakistani terrorists to attack Shivaratri celebrations in the Indian state of Gujarat. Janjua told Doval that ten suicide terrorists from Lashkar-e-Taiba and Jaish-e-Muhammad had entered Gujarat with plans of a series of attacks similar to those that left 166 civilians dead in Mumbai in November 2008.[1]

The Pakistani warning resulted in massive mobilization of security services in Gujarat. Four teams of the National Security Guard (NSG) were stationed at Ahmedabad airport, armed police moved to protect vital installations and public areas, and the historic Somnath temple was turned into a fortress to ward off would-be attackers. Similar security measures were put in place in Delhi, just in case the terrorists targeted the Indian capital instead of Gujarat.[2]

In the end, Shivaratri passed without terrorist attacks. Pakistan's decision to share intelligence was likely related to Indian and American pressure following January's terrorist attacks on the Pathankot air force base in Indian Punjab. India had cancelled scheduled talks in response to the attack and Pakistan's Prime Minister Nawaz Sharif was eager to resume dialogue. Diplomats in Delhi described the Pakistani gesture as an effort 'to preempt a potential crisis in bilateral relations, even war'.[3] That it reflected genuine concern for possible Indian casualties was less likely. Jihadist blogs in Pakistan accused the civilian government of selling out to India by sharing intelligence that might enable India to target Al-Qaeda in the Indian subcontinent, with one article claiming that Janjua had earlier also conveyed information that allowed India to shut down a terror cell in December 2015.

The assault on Pathankot air base that began on 2 January 2016 threatened to derail a thaw in India–

Pakistan ties marked by Prime Minister Narendra Modi's stopover in Lahore on Christmas Day barely a week earlier. Indians were shocked that a group of gunmen, dressed in Indian army uniforms, engaged Indian troops in a battle that raged for three days at an air base about 35 kilometres from the border with Pakistan. Initially, the anti-India Kashmiri militant alliance, the United Jihad Council (UJC), took credit for the assault, but Indian intelligence pinned the blame on Jaish-e-Muhammad, one of seventy-two terrorist groups that continue to operate despite being officially banned in Pakistan.

Modi demanded Pakistan's immediate response to the attack, and Sharif agreed to investigate the Pathankot attackers' Pakistani links. Both leaders were eager not to jeopardize the dialogue they had only recently revived. Soon after that, Pakistani intelligence agencies sought more evidence about Pathankot, while the Pakistani media hinted that India was accusing Pakistan falsely. Five cellphone numbers used for making calls from Pakistan to India, provided by Indian authorities, were reportedly unregistered and had fake identities.[4] India decided to allow a Pakistani investigation team to come to the Pathankot base, expecting that this would be seen as evidence of a genuine desire to get to the bottom of the matter. As enemies, India and Pakistan do not normally provide each other's intelligence officers access to their military bases.

The attempts at joint investigation did not, however, have the desired result of solving the puzzle. Instead, Pakistani newspapers reported that the Pakistani investigation team saw the attack as a tool for India's 'vicious propaganda' against Pakistan 'without having any solid evidence to back the claim'. [5] The Indians insisted they had offered evidence that the Pathankot attack was planned in Pakistan and that Pakistani officials did not contradict that evidence.[6]

Public expressions of goodwill and cooperation notwithstanding, the investigation and the subsequent Pakistani help in averting a terrorist attack in Gujarat stalled in their tracks. Pakistan announced that it had arrested an Indian spy who had admitted to supporting terrorism in Pakistan's Balochistan province and Karachi. In April 2016 Pakistan announced that dialogue with India had been suspended because of India's actions against Pakistan. An opportunity to work together against terrorists was reduced to another battle in the unending public relations war that has run parallel to rampant terrorist violence on both sides of the border.

Warnings about a possible attack in Gujarat were not the first time India and Pakistan had exchanged intelligence about impending terrorist attacks on each other's soil. More than a decade earlier, India's external intelligence service Research and Analysis Wing (R&AW) communicated information obtained from intercepted phone calls about a planned 15 December 2003 assassination attempt on Pakistan's then president, General Pervez Musharraf. The ISI decided to let the attack go ahead so that it could identify and trace the perpetrators, but the Indian forewarning enabled Pakistani security forces to protect Musharraf when the attack occurred.

Janjua and Doval had opened a direct channel, which led to the Gujarat warning, but the heads of Pakistani and Indian intelligence had done so much earlier, when they had begun meeting secretly in the summer of 2003 to reduce terrorism across the Line of Control in Jammu and

Kashmir. The intelligence sharing that saved Musharraf's life was the result of communications between C.D. Sahay, head of R&AW, and Lt Gen. Ehsan-ul-Haq, chief of the ISI. Meetings between Haq and Sahay in third countries also resulted in an unwritten ceasefire along the Line of Control in Jammu and Kashmir, enabling India to fence-off terrorist infiltration routes.

The effort at intelligence sharing that began with the US prodding of Musharraf and Vajpayee in 2003 did not, however, lead to prosecution of Pakistani terrorists in India. Both sides eventually felt there was little exchange of usable intelligence, and the arrangement, or whatever little there was of one, collapsed after the 26/11 attacks in Mumbai five years later.

An earlier effort in 1987, involving a secret meeting in Switzerland between R&AW chief A.K. Verma and his Pakistani counterpart, Lt Gen. Hamid Gul, had collapsed with the beginning of militant insurgency in Jammu and Kashmir. Verma and Gul had met at the behest of Pakistan's dictator General Zia-ul-Haq and Indian Prime Minister Rajiv Gandhi. Their objective had ostensibly been to diminish the risk of war that India felt had been created by Pakistan's support for the Khalistan insurgency in Indian Punjab.[7]

The fact is, the ISI and R&AW simply do not trust each other enough for the two intelligence services to consistently exchange intelligence about likely terrorist attacks. In the ISI's worldview, R&AW caused Pakistan's break-up in 1971 by supporting Bengali nationalists, and wants to repeat its success in Sindh, Balochistan and Khyber-Pashtunkhwa. For R&AW, it is the ISI's repeated use of terrorism and its efforts to encircle India through covert operations in neighbouring countries that perpetuates the India–Pakistan conflict. Both agencies have played 'Spy versus Spy' for several decades.

India's role in helping Bangladesh win independence, including the role of R&AW, is well documented. Equally well documented is the ill-treatment of Bengalis by Pakistan's Punjab-based leaders, which paved the way for plans by R&AW's founding chief, Rameshwar Nath Kao, to train and equip the Bangladesh liberation army, the Mukti Bahini. The lesson to be learned from the Bangladesh war should have been to avoid creating disgruntled citizens who might become insurgents trained by a hostile neighbour.

Instead, Pakistan's generals since 1971 have wanted only to avenge their defeat by somehow replicating India's covert war success in Bangladesh. Every now and then some Indians, too, want to repeat their earlier triumph, though changes in global politics and the introduction of nuclear weapons in the subcontinent now make that virtually impossible. The Mukti Bahini took over Bangladesh's countryside but the Pakistan army's control of cities ended only at the hands of the Indian army. Neither country can now execute a similar stratagem without risking nuclear war.

As a consequence, India and Pakistan are mired in proxy wars that, unlike the outcome in Bangladesh, have failed to come to a decisive end. India, and much of the world, accuses Pakistan of nurturing jihadi terrorists as an instrument of policy, flexing muscle to advance Pakistan's strategic goals against Afghanistan and India. Although Pakistan denies any involvement, making different arguments at different times, there is little doubt that anti-India terrorists have received funding and training in Pakistan. Pakistan's excuses that terrorists represent genuine grievances of Kashmiris, Muslims and other minorities oppressed by India have few takers outside Pakistan. Claims that India orchestrates terrorist attacks against itself just to be able to blame Pakistan are often laughed off in the world's capitals even though many Pakistanis earnestly believe them.

Both India and Pakistan have been victims of terrorist attacks over the last twenty-five years, most (but not all) of which stem from the India–Pakistan discord. It is plausible that India covertly supports radical ethnic movements in parts of Pakistan though, despite complaining about it for years, Pakistan has not been able to present evidence about Indian subversion that might convince the rest of the world. Pakistan, on the other hand, has been accused by the international community of funding, arming, training and maintaining large groups of militants who often operate freely and with support from the state apparatus.

According to the South Asia Terrorism Portal, which tracks all incidents of terrorism and violence in the region, 64,916 people were killed in political violence in India between 1994 and March 2016, including 24,688 civilians, 9731 security force personnel and 30,497 terrorists. This violence involved Kashmiri jihadists and other Islamists, Hindutva extremists, Maoist insurgents, North-East rebels and violent Khalistan militants in Punjab.[8] More than two-thirds of these fatalities occurred as a result of bloodshed in Jammu and Kashmir, where 47,234 terrorist incidents have been recorded since 1988. Indian officials have reported the death of 14,725 civilians, 6193 security force personnel and 22,996 terrorists in Jammu and Kashmir during the same period.[9]

Pakistan has also lost 60,388 lives to terrorism since 2003, when Islamist terrorists started targeting their own country. Until 10 April 2016, civilians accounted for 21,083 terrorism- related deaths, while 6454 security force personnel and 32,851 terrorists were also reportedly killed.[10] Pakistan has also witnessed 3020 incidents of sectarian terrorism since 1989, involving mainly extremist Sunni jihadi groups targeting Shias and Ahmadis, resulting in more than 5000 deaths.[11]

Most people trace the rise of jihadi terrorism to the anti-Soviet war in Afghanistan (1979–88) and the militant agitation that began in Jammu and Kashmir from 1989 in reaction to Delhi's interference in state politics, especially the rigging of state elections in 1987. In Pakistan's strategic thinking, however, the idea of using irregular warfare as an equalizer against a much larger India dates back to at least the late 1950s. Pakistan had used tribal militias in Jammu and Kashmir as early as 1948 but at that time Pakistan had no clear military doctrine. Over time, the idea of irregular warfare has been gradually expanded to include support for various insurgencies and terrorist attacks. Being smaller than India, Pakistan cannot succeed in a conventional military offensive but it hopes to force India's hand by disrupting life in its cities and creating fear all round.

In 1958 Field Marshal Ayub Khan boasted of Pakistan's 'proven and trusted manpower that can do the fighting' while telling Americans that they needed to furnish the Pakistani armed forces with modern equipment.[12] Aslam Siddiqi, an official in Ayub's Bureau of National Reconstruction, added that Pakistan must prepare for the day its alliance with the US ends by turning 'to its own ideology and inner strength', and advocated jihad through unofficial militias. 'In its manpower Pakistan is very fortunate,' he wrote, reminding Pakistanis of their 'traditions of irregular fighting'. Instead of depending solely on a well-equipped regular army, 'why not train irregular fighters whom even the existing industries of Pakistan can well equip?' Siddiqi suggested.[13]

Siddiqi's doctrine of 'irregular warfare' spoke of 'spreading out and prolonging action'. Its essence was 'to deny the enemy any target and to keep attacking him again at unexpected places'.[14] In his view, the dogma of war for Pakistan entailed a marriage between the irregular fighter and the regular soldier – something that was first tried methodically by Pakistan in the prelude to the 1965 war. Then, irregular forces were expected to generate a popular uprising in the Kashmir Valley, paving the way for regular Pakistani troops who would follow to take and hold territory.

The doctrine received a shot in the arm during the 1980s, when the United States decided to bleed the Soviet Union in Afghanistan by supporting Pakistan-based mujahideen. The Afghan jihad brought to Pakistan substantial amounts of money, weapons and fighters from all over the world. Pakistanis trained alongside Arab and Afghan mujahideen, all of whom learned new and varied methods of sabotage and bomb-making techniques.[15] Pakistan's security establishment diverted some of these techniques to assist Sikhs involved in the Khalistan insurgency. A major advantage of the 'hit-terrorize-run or die' approach to irregular warfare was that it did not require direct involvement in conflict of regular forces. Just as the Afghans bled the Soviets to the point where the Soviets opted to withdraw, it was assumed that the new jihadi or Khalsa would inflict sufficient pain on India to force surrender.

The political situation following the March 1987 Jammu and Kashmir state assembly elections presented an opportunity for Pakistan's stirring of the pot. The ruling coalition comprising the Jammu and Kashmir National Conference led by Farooq Abdullah and the Indian National Congress (I) were challenged in the election by a combination of secessionist and pro-Pakistan groups named the Muslim United Front (MUF) that contested these elections. The MUF won only eight of the seventy-six state assembly seats even though it polled 34 per cent of the votes along with independents.[16] The ruling coalition won sixty-six seats, leading most analysts even in India to conclude that the outcome of these elections reflected rigging.

Protests broke out in the Kashmir Valley soon after the disputed state election. Pakistani intelligence agents recruited discontented Kashmiri youth for full-blown militancy against India. Over time Pakistani jihadi groups replaced the ones led by Kashmiris to expand the scope of fighting.

For years, Pakistan officially argued that it did not see militancy in Jammu and Kashmir as terrorism. According to Islamabad, the state was disputed territory and, therefore, its insurgency against Indian rule was part of the Kashmiri people's freedom struggle. That argument lost weight once ISI shifted support away from Kashmiri groups such as the Jammu and Kashmir Liberation Front and Hizbul Mujahideen to Pakistani jihadi groups such as Harkat-ul-Ansar, Harkat-ul-Mujahideen, Lashkar-e-Taiba and Jaish-e-Muhammad.

Moreover, after initially focusing on attacks inside the Kashmir Valley, the Pakistani groups expanded their operations to other parts of India. Kidnapping of westerners in 1993 and hijacking of an Indian Airlines aircraft to Kandahar in 1999 demolished the legitimacy of the 'freedom fighter, not terrorists' argument. The case collapsed completely after Lashkar-e-Taiba's attack on the Indian parliament in December 2001, when international public opinion turned against Pakistan's support of even Kashmir-oriented militant groups. Several Pakistani groups are now listed among terrorist groups facing sanctions from the United Nations, the European Union, the United States as well as influential Muslim countries such as Saudi Arabia and the UAE.

Pakistan adopted terrorism as a low-cost means of bleeding India, assuming that it could replicate what many nations had together done against the Soviets in Afghanistan. The Soviets withdrew from Afghanistan because the cost of staying there outweighed any benefits. That has not applied in India's case. Indians could not pack up and leave Kashmir, which to them was a part of their country. The Pakistani assumption that India would see Jammu and Kashmir as a dispensable appendage, like the Soviets saw Afghanistan, turned out to be flawed.

The expansion of jihad, meanwhile, has disrupted Pakistani society. It has empowered extremist Pakistani mullahs seeking greater power at home in the name of Islamization. Armed militias, which is what the anti-India jihadi groups are, are a danger to any society. At the height of the jihad in Kashmir, groups like Lashkar-e-Taiba advertised telephone numbers in major Pakistani cities that students on summer break could call to join jihad, part-time. Some of the young men thus trained have been responsible for self-motivated attacks – such as the targeted killing of the Karachi social activist Sabeen Mahmud for celebrating Valentine's Day, and the attempt on the life of Nobel laureate Malala Yusufzai for posting blogs against Taliban opposition to girls' schooling. Such attacks do not advance anybody's strategic interests.

Ideologically motivated jihadi militancy is not a tap that can be turned on or off by the government at will. Many of the irregular warriors recruited for terrorism join jihad for religious reasons. Theological arguments were used to motivate them to fight India, and these have also turned some of them against the Pakistani state. For example, Hadith (sayings attributed to Prophet Muhammad) about a final battle in 'Hind' before the end of times, which were once a staple for recruitment by Pakistani jihadi groups, are now being interpreted by more extreme offshoots to target Pakistan and its army.

Throughout the 1990s, Pakistani official media encouraged discussion of these 'Ghazwa-e-Hind' Hadith to motivate jihadists. Every major Pakistan-based jihadi group that launched terrorist attacks across the border claimed that their operations were part of the Battle for India promised by Islam's Prophet. These ISI-backed groups saw the modern state of India and its 'occupation' of Kashmir as targets of jihad. However, some extremist groups (such as Tehrik-e-Taliban Pakistan – TTP) interpret 'Hind' mentioned in the Hadith as historic India, which includes modern Pakistan. These groups consider terrorist attacks inside Pakistan as a legitimate part of their effort to erode western influence inside Pakistan.

Attacks inside Pakistan have forced the Pakistan army to fight certain jihadi groups. Many Pakistanis realize that the country's embrace of terrorism as strategy has rebounded; it endangers the lives of Pakistanis, engenders lawlessness and makes Pakistan a potential international pariah. Still, Pakistan's generals remain fundamentally wedded to the idea of irregular warfare.

'India has its limitations and serious ones at that,' observed Major General Amin Khan Burki, commandant of the army's Command and Staff College, complaining that the international media dubiously built up India's image as the dominant regional power. He added that 'Taken in its totality, including its limitations, India will be cut to its proper size and dimension, that is only quasi powerful and very much a manageable military power.'[17]

'Cutting India down to size' is not a mere figure of speech; it has for years been an active policy backed by irregular warfare. Pakistani military officers are told that 'India was hostage to a centrifugal rather than a centripetal tradition'[18] and had a 'historical inability to exist as a single unified state'.[19] The temptation to avenge the humiliation of losing Pakistan's erstwhile eastern wing by forcing India to go through something similar outweighs the concerns sensible Pakistanis have about jihadism's negative consequences for our own country. Pakistan still has an unfinished strategic agenda in Afghanistan and Kashmir and, given its lack of military and economic strength, irregular warfare with the help of Islamists remains, in the generals' view, a cheap and easy option.

India has alternated between engaging Pakistan and trying to 'name and shame' it internationally as a terrorism incubator. The length and depth of engagement through talks has not been enough to reassure Pakistan that India does not mean harm. India's attempts to isolate Pakistan have only aggravated Pakistan's fears about Indian conspiracies. The result is exacerbation of irregular warfare, without raising the international cost of that strategy to levels that Pakistan might not be able to sustain. India could, but has so far been unable to, reach out to the Pakistani people and convince them that it does not seek Pakistan's break-up and only seeks good neighbourly ties. Such an effort would require sustained engagement and outreach, which India's domestic politics often renders difficult.

I realized the pitfalls of Pakistan's policy on jihadi terrorism years before terrorist attacks inside Pakistan woke up my countrymen to its dangers. US Secretary of State Hillary Clinton told Pakistanis publicly in October 2011: 'You can't keep snakes in your backyard and expect them only to bite your neighbors.' That was almost two decades after another US secretary of state, James A.

Baker III, warned Pakistan about the prospect of being designated a state sponsor of terrorism. As special assistant to then prime minister Nawaz Sharif in 1991–92, I was involved in negotiations with the administration of President George H.W. Bush that gave me an insight into our snake-rearing as well as its potential consequences.

Baker wrote a rather terse letter to Sharif in May 1992, which was delivered by US Ambassador Nicholas Platt, who also provided a copy to me. It demanded that Pakistan take 'steps to make certain that Kashmiri and Sikh groups and individuals who have committed acts of terrorism do not receive support from Pakistani officials'. Baker noted Pakistani assurances that 'by later this year Pakistan will take steps to distance itself from terrorist activities against India', and that 'the training which outsiders, including Kashmiris, previously received alongside Afghan mujahideen in Pakistan is being halted'.

According to Baker, the US had 'information indicating that ISI and others intend to continue to provide material support to groups that have engaged in terrorism'. He warned that he took such information very seriously because 'US law requires that an onerous package of sanctions apply to those states found to be supporting such acts of international terrorism.' The US secretary of state urged the Pakistani prime minister 'to affirm that the Government of Pakistan assumes full responsibility for ensuring that no training, weapons or other support is provided in Pakistan or Azad Kashmir to Kashmiri or Sikh groups that have engaged in terrorism'. He also asked that Sharif 'block efforts to shift training elsewhere, such as just across the border in Afghanistan'.[20]

The Americans knew not only the full extent of Pakistan's involvement with jihadi terrorism but were also aware of future plans. At that time, Pakistan's jihadi infrastructure had not yet come out in the open. Lashkar-e-Taiba, with its sprawling 200-acre compound in Muridke near Lahore, and Jaish-e-Muhammad's ambitious madrasa near Bahawalpur had yet to make their appearance. Pakistan, however, was already running the risk of international isolation and the sanctions that come with being declared a state sponsor of terrorism.

Sharif's reply to Baker took several days to draft, with the foreign office, ISI and the Pakistan army all weighing in on its contents. In the end, the letter dated 20 June 1992 was delivered in Washington DC four days later by the minister of state for foreign affairs, Siddiq Khan Kanju. A quarter-century later, the letter (the contents of which have not been published to date) summarizes Pakistan's denial as well as explains its rationale for its continued involvement with anti-Indian terrorism:

'Pakistan and the United States have a long history of relations based on trust and friendship,' Sharif wrote, listing Pakistan's 'services' to the United States. 'We were allies when communism threatened the fundamental values that we share, indeed the very basis of our existence. Pakistan was glad to play a helpful role in the revival of your relations with China, which altered the strategic balance of the world. In Afghanistan and in the Gulf, we stood shoulder to shoulder in defense of fundamental principles of the UN Charter. In our foreign policy, we seek international and regional peace through moderation. Internally, we share a commitment to upholding the basic freedoms of democracy and human rights. I greatly value these ties.'

Then he went on to list Pakistani grievances: 'Yet I cannot help feeling a sense of disappointment that despite this close association and sharing of perceptions, the balance of goodwill, as seen from the United States, is recently weighed against us. Given this long and resonant association, I feel we can expect a fair and even handed attitude from the United States. For instance, when Pakistan is accused of assisting terrorism in Kashmir and Punjab, silence on the state terrorism being carried out by the Indian government in Kashmir is difficult to understand.'

Sharif followed up with Pakistan's assertions against India on Kashmir. 'Indian suppression has gone beyond the denial of human rights and now encompasses arson, torture, rape and killings that have reached a figure of 6000,' he wrote. 'Moreover, government sponsored agents from India have perpetrated a campaign of terror through subversion and sabotage in Pakistan's provinces of Sind and Punjab. Several Indian intelligence agents have been caught red-handed and have admitted their guilt. We have clear evidence of their acts of terrorism as also of the government-sponsored media campaign.'

Commitments and assurances came next. 'I assure you that my government is firmly opposed to terrorism in all its forms,' continued the letter. 'On a number of occasions we have demonstrated this commitment. In February of this year we killed our own people in order to stop their crossing the line of control in Kashmir. We do support the Kashmiri people's struggle for self-determination but our support is and will remain moral, political and diplomatic. Indeed, so strong is the Kashmiri case and so just is their cause that recourse to terrorism would only harm it.'

'The commitments made to Ambassador Burleigh when he visited Pakistan will be met,' Sharif promised, referring to verbal assurances regarding specific steps to be taken by Pakistan. 'All agencies of the Government of Pakistan are under strict orders to ensure that no training for terrorist activities or assistance for infiltration into Indian Kashmir is provided. Unlike India which has denied access to the international media and representatives of the humanitarian agencies from visiting Indian held Kashmir to witness the gross human rights violations in that area, Pakistan would welcome any such groups or observers to satisfy themselves that there are no camps in Pakistan for training or infiltrating suspect elements.'

Denial followed the promises once again. 'As regards the Indian province of Punjab, its problems unlike Kashmir, are internal to India,' the letter went on. 'The Government of India must resolve these problems in whatever fashion it chooses. We have no interest in colluding with Sikh activists or extending assistance to them. Pakistan remains committed to the principle of non-interference in the internal affairs of other states and expects India to observe the same principle with respect to our territory.'

Sharif's letter to Secretary of State Baker closed with a solemn pledge. 'I hope that the assurances that I am conveying to you will remove any doubts regarding our intentions and actions. I would be grateful for any information which indicates evidence to the contrary as it would help me stamp out any unauthorized activity in contravention of express orders.'

'Allow me to conclude that Pakistan has long admired United States' strong support for the observance of human rights,' Sharif continued. 'We have been deeply impressed by your country's commitment to the principle of self-determination of peoples. These principles are being violated with impunity in Kashmir and insistence of their observance is the duty of all those who regard them as sacrosanct. We believe that the United States can exercise its moral and political influence to help resolve the core issue of Kashmir which has remained the basic cause of tension and confrontation between Pakistan and India and the breeding ground of violence and suppression of human rights.'[21]

A few months after writing that letter, Sharif was removed from office in military-backed political manoeuvres. He was succeeded as prime minister by Benazir Bhutto, whom the Americans initially considered more credible than Sharif in keeping promises. The Americans removed the threat of sanctions though they continued to complain about terrorism. The jihad in Kashmir became more ferocious over time, even more so when Sharif succeeded Bhutto after another palace coup. Eventually, General Pervez Musharraf overthrew Sharif in October 1999 and the military ran Pakistan directly for the succeeding nine years.

An ISI briefing to Sharif around the time of the US threats about declaring Pakistan a state sponsor of terrorism laid out the ISI's understanding of India's intentions about Pakistan, which it then matches with irregular warfare. 'Research and Analysis Wing of Indian intelligence network is the third dimension of India's foreign policy manifestation aimed at conducting clandestine operations across the borders,' said the ISI briefing paper. 'The Objectives of RAW against Pakistan are: To divide Pakistan on ethnic and sectarian basis; To disprove and ridicule the "Two Nation Theory"; Weaken Pakistan to an extent that it ceases to pose any threat to Indian hegemonic designs; Involve Pakistan army into internal security to the extent that its attention across the borders gets divided and ultimately destroyed; To destabilize Sindh with a view to counter Khalistan and Kashmir movements.'

The ISI listed R&AW's operating techniques as: 'Attacking the minds of target audience through subversive themes. Technique used is through electronic and print media, printed material in form of newspapers, magazines and pamphlets; exploitation of ethnic, cultural, economic and political grounds; controlling covert operations through cover appointments in Indian

Embassy/Indian consulate; financial support to dissident elements, agents and surrogates; through recruitment of "key communicators" or "agents of influence"; training and arming of agents/dissident elements and infiltrating them back to target country.'[22]

In the ISI's view, jihadi terrorism only counters R&AW's operations to weaken Pakistan's ideology by trying to cut India down to size. There is no evidence that ISI's understanding of India–Pakistan relations has changed since that briefing decades ago. Pakistan's Islamists, and a large number of civilian Pakistanis, also embrace this version of Pakistani nationalism focused on the imaginary threat from India. As long as the belief exists that Pakistan must undermine India before India does the same to Pakistan, it is unlikely that terrorism will stop being an issue in the subcontinent.

Every time I read official Pakistani pronouncements about terrorism, I am reminded of Sharif's 1992 letter to the US government painstakingly written by Pakistan's civil and military officials, general and politicians together. I did not participate in writing that letter, which comprises inexactitudes, false promises and a narration of grievances that remains central to Pakistani policy to this day. Nothing Pakistani officials have said since then differs substantively from what Sharif conveyed to Baker in that letter.

Although Pakistan has not been targeted with sanctions, its standing in the international community has diminished considerably. Pakistani travellers to foreign lands are subjected to much greater scrutiny because of fears of terrorism. And the country also bears the brunt of terrorist attacks on its soil and the consequent economic and social costs. But the forward policy of containing India's potential subversion of Pakistan through subversion endures, even at great risk of blowback on Pakistan.

Following the 9/11 terrorist attacks in the United States in 2001, Musharraf was forced to ban some militant groups and declare that he would not allow terrorism, even in the name of Kashmir. Fifteen years later, that promise rings hollow. Groups are banned only to resurface under new names while prominent terrorist masterminds are almost always set free by Pakistani courts. Jihad is officially put on hold sometimes but it is never completely rolled back.

Soon after the Mumbai attacks, US Secretary of State Condoleezza Rice told Pakistan's national security adviser, Major General Mahmud Durrani, in my presence that Pakistan had all the information it needed to shut terrorist operations down forever. After all, ISI knew who it had trained and equipped for terrorism. 'I realize that there could be instability if you go after the jihadis groups,' she observed, 'but you will be consumed if you do not.' It seemed that she felt the need to convey her strongly held views before she ended her tenure. She had been diplomatic with Pakistani officials for eight years, but now she wanted to get it out.

Rice said, 'Focusing your energies on an Indian threat that does not exist is a colossal mistake.' Pakistan had to 'make a strategic decision that association with terrorists has to come to an end'. According to her, Pakistan could not 'keep these people as an option' because 'keeping contacts with various jihadi groups is not acceptable'. She said the United States and Britain would help if Pakistan lacked the capacity to take on the terrorists.

ISI chief Lt Gen. Ahmed Shuja Pasha then visited the United States for a meeting with the CIA director

Michael Hayden. In his most recent book, *Playing to the Edge*, Hayden wrote that 'duplicitous' was a gentler way to describe the ISI and its close links with terror groups.[23] During his meeting with Hayden after the Mumbai attacks, Pasha admitted that the planners of the Mumbai attacks included some 'retired Pakistani army officers'. According to Pasha, the attackers had ISI links, but this had not been an authorized ISI operation.

At my official residence as Pakistan's ambassador to the United States, Pasha said to me in Urdu, *'Loag hamaray thay, operation hamara nahin thha'* (The people involved in the Mumbai attack were ours but it was not our operation). I asked him, *'Agar hamaray loag bhi hamaray qaboo mein nahin tau aagay kya hoga?'* (If we have no control over our own people, what is our future?) That question still awaits a well-thought-out answer.

5

The Space for Friendship
Is Shrinking

Sixty-nine years after Partition it is hard to believe that Gandhi wanted to treat Pakistan as an estranged brother or that Jinnah wanted to retire in India after serving as Governor-General of Pakistan. Most of the subcontinent's current population – 94 per cent of Indians, 95.5 per cent of Pakistanis – were born after Independence in 1947. Yet, the anger and rhetoric of Partition forms part of transmitted memories while the reconciliatory statements by Gandhi and Jinnah after Partition do not.

Indians, beginning with Nehru and Patel, chose to punish Pakistan for breaking away instead of wooing it. In doing so they reinforced the effort by Jinnah's successors to militarize and Islamize Pakistan. The new country, burdened by the inheritance of a larger military than economy, ended up building its identity through opposition to India. Pakistanis chose to invent a version of history that stretched Hindu–Muslim rivalry over centuries, casting the two communities as irreconcilable enemies. The Kashmir dispute, terrorism and the advent of nuclear weapons in the subcontinent have all aggravated that rivalry.

In Pakistan's case, treating India just as a neighbouring state has proved difficult because of India's centrality to Pakistan's identity as a separate nation. Indians often think that it helps if they accentuate similarities between the two countries but actually it scares Pakistanis even more. India's evolution as a secular country with almost as many Muslims as Pakistan also feeds mistrust, which in turn fuels the need to emphasize differences.

An ostensibly liberal Pakistani official summarized Pakistan's dilemma by asking an American reporter in 1980, 'If we are not Muslims, what are we, second-rate Indians?'[1] This desire not to be Indians had also dominated the deliberations of the First Congress on the History and Culture of Pakistan held at Islamabad University in 1973, in the aftermath of the loss of Bangladesh. The conference proceedings were published as *The Quest for Identity*. The prominent Pakistani academic Waheed-uz-Zaman stated in his editor's note, 'If the Arabs, the Turks, the Iranians, God forbid, give up Islam, the Arabs yet remain Arabs, the Turks remain Turks, the Iranians remain Iranians, but what do we remain if we give up Islam?'[2]

Islam and anti-India sentiment are the cornerstones of the 'ideology of Pakistan', which effectively claims for the current Pakistani state the mantle of successor to the Sultans of Delhi or the Mughal emperors. Addressing the UN Security Council during the 1965 war as Pakistan's foreign minister, Zulfikar Ali Bhutto spoke of Indian leaders seeing Pakistan as their 'Enemy number one', 'the fulcrum of India's fundamental policies'. Representatives of other countries were surprised when he said that 'For seven hundred years we sought to achieve equilibrium between the people of the two major communities', given that Pakistan had existed only for eighteen years at the time.[3]

Instead of refuting an incorrect narrative of history and tempering Pakistani paranoia, some Indians chose to exacerbate it. In the process, a fear of India's disintegration at Pakistan's hands was born. 'In Pakistan's view the Partition is only the beginning,' Nehru's defence minister Krishna Menon once told a British interviewer. 'Her idea is to get a jumping-off ground to take the whole of India,' he said, claiming that he knew the way Pakistani minds worked. According to Krishna Menon, Pakistanis believe that 'it was from the Mughals that the British took over. Now the British having gone, they must come back.'⁴ Arguments by Pakistani military officers about India being incapable of building a unified state play into that fear.

India's harsh perception of Pakistan is thus encapsulated by India's former national security adviser and foreign secretary J.N. Dixit: 'The reason Britain partitioned India was to fragment Hindu areas into political entities and ensure Pakistan's emergence as the largest and most cohesive political power in the subcontinent. Pakistan's ultimate aim is to fragment India. Pakistani invasion of Kashmir in 1948 and subsequent wars are a part of this continuous exercise. The Kargil war and the proxy war in Jammu and Kashmir are the latest example of this pressure. India has not been decisive and surgical in resisting Pakistani subversion. India has voluntarily given concessions to Pakistan despite defeating it in all the major conflicts. Pakistan's long-term strategic objective is to ensure that India does not emerge as the most influential power in the South Asian region. The Pakistani power structure has a powerful antagonism towards Hindu-majority civil society in India. Pakistan has sought the support of a large number of Muslim countries and Asian and Western powers (China and the US) to keep India on the defensive. Pakistan's continued questioning of Indian secularism, democracy and constitutional institutions is a deliberate attempt to generate friction within India. Pakistani support to secessionist and insurgent forces in Jammu and Kashmir, in Punjab and in the north- eastern states of India confirms this impression.'5

Characterizations of the Indian mind as being full of hate towards Muslims, of the Pakistani mind as wanting to break up India, and the two sides being eternal enemies render normal diplomatic negotiations impossible. Such stereotypes defy logic. After all, how can one billion people have one way of thinking and how can Islam pit Pakistan's 200 million Muslims against India, while 180 million Indian Muslims and another billion around the world are not necessarily India's enemies? US President Dwight Eisenhower had once remarked, 'There was no problem between Pakistan and India which could not be solved if both countries approached it with reason and good will.' However, it is difficult to have reason and good will when emotions, stereotypes and fear dominate the relationship.

These emotions and fear have been reinforced over generations by means of education that has amounted to virtual indoctrination. The Pakistani historian K.K. Aziz describes Pakistani textbooks as being replete with historical errors and suggests that their mandatory study amounted to the teaching of 'prescribed myths'.[6] After examining sixty-six textbooks for social studies and Pakistan studies – mandatory subjects at different levels of schooling – Aziz argued that these textbooks aimed at supporting military rule in Pakistan, inculcating hatred for Hindus, glorifying wars and distorting the pre-1947 history of the area comprising Pakistan.[7]

According to Aziz, beginning with elementary school, Pakistani students are taught to believe that 'Pakistan was a fortress of Islam'; 'the advent of Islam reformed Hindu society'; 'the Muslims came to this country, bringing with them a clean and elegant culture and civilization... The Hindus are indeed indebted to Muslim culture and civilization today'; and 'The Hindus wanted to control the government of India after independence. The British sided with the Hindus but the Muslims did not accept this decision.'

Although Pakistan had emerged through a complex process of negotiations, and between 1858 and 1929 as many as sixty-four different schemes had been proposed for protecting the rights of Muslims in British India, Pakistani students are provided a simplified history. Every Pakistani textbook 'insists and reiterates that Islam was the first premise of the syllogism of the Pakistan demand; Islam cannot co-exist with Hinduism, therefore Muslims must separate from India; ergo, Pakistan must be created'.[8]

Some books go so far as to suggest that the idea of Pakistan was born the day the first Muslim conqueror set foot in India, without acknowledging earlier Muslim communities of traders and sailors along the South Indian coast that predated the Muslim warriors and conquerors. Pakistan's history is thus stretched back to the eighth-century conquest of a part of modern Pakistan by Umayyad general Muhammad bin Qasim. Traditional ulema are described as being the founders of the ideology of Pakistan even when they had no direct role in the pre-Independence history of the country. Jinnah's post-Independence attempts at mitigating communalism with a more secular outlook for the country he founded are not even mentioned.

The tendentious historical narrative does not end merely with arguing in favour of Pakistan's justification. The communal riots at the time of Partition are described as 'Hindu and Sikh massacres of unarmed Muslims'. The 1965 war with India is described as a Pakistani victory, which ended only when 'India sued for peace' because it was 'frightened of the Pakistan army and the people of Pakistan'. The separation of East Pakistan is explained away as the result of collaboration between Pakistan's 'external and internal enemies' and 'Indian aggression'. Young Pakistanis are taught that patriotism is the same thing as xenophobia. Pakistan is constantly under threat and only militarism and militancy can protect it.

In recent years, India and Pakistan are increasingly resembling each other in rage, resentment and public displays of religion. At the time of Partition, all sides committed acts of violence but at least India's mainstream leaders stood up to declare that the people of the subcontinent are members of one family. Even as Pakistan got engulfed in debates about an 'Islamic' constitution and Islamization of laws, India's Constitution expressly declared the country as a secular state.

One-third of the subcontinent's Muslims stayed on in India even after Pakistan's creation. The virtual cleansing of Hindus and Sikhs from what was then West Pakistan diminished the percentage of non-Muslims in today's Pakistan to 3 per cent.[9] But the percentage of Muslims in India actually increased, to about 14 per cent of the population. While Lahore's Lakshmi Chowk was replaced with a Muslim name, at least Delhi retained its Akbar and Shahjahan Roads. Secular Pakistanis, opposed to the travesties perpetrated in the name of Islam in their own country, often cited India as a flawed but still desirable model of pluralism.

That is less and less the case now. Things have gradually

changed in India, to the detriment of the argument within Pakistan for a pluralist Pakistan. And the impact of these developments on India–Pakistan relations can't be positive.

Passions, fuelled by firebrands, distorted accounts of history and violence that begets further violence, are shrinking whatever little space has existed for friendship between India and Pakistan. Instead, they are spilling over into the Hindu–Muslim relationship within India, with potential for 'we told you so' arguments in Pakistan by radical Islamists who have built an ideology of permanent hate towards India and Hindus on the edifice of the two-nation theory.

Differences between a 'secular India' and a 'semi-theocratic' Pakistan are still obvious but they are looking less pronounced.

In Pakistan, the military's dominance can be held responsible for feeding the frenzy of eternal war between two neighbouring countries that until 1947 were one. The military–intelligence combine that has effectively run Pakistan has hounded the advocates of peace with India. Pakistani textbooks, beginning with Ayub Khan's military regime (1958–69), have passed on a contrived historical narrative and expanded the emphasis on an exclusivist version of Islam. Pakistan's ministry of information and the military's psychological warfare experts have ensured that a message similar to the one taught at schools is available to grown-ups through radio, television, films, magazines, books and newspapers.

On the Indian side, invention of Indian nationalism under Congress governments made Indians oblivious to the fact that India was more a civilization than a single nation state for most of its history. The pre-Partition political battle between the Congress and the Muslim League was often painted in such stark terms that it aroused anger rather than understanding of that era's politics.

More recently, the attempts to saffronize the curriculum have also encouraged chauvinism. There have been suggestions that maps of India at schools should include 'countries like Pakistan, Afghanistan, Nepal, Bhutan, Tibet, Bangladesh, Sri Lanka and Burma' as they are all 'part of Akhand Bharat'. Young minds are being exposed to statements such as 'undivided India is the truth, divided India is a lie. Division of India is unnatural and it can be united again'.[10] There is an absence of nuanced discussion of history and interstate relations, which is needed if India is to fulfil its ambition of being a major global power.

Nehru wrote to Patel as early as 1950 that he deplored the 'constant cry for retaliation and of vicarious punishment of the Muslims of India, because the Pakistanis punish Hindus. That argument does not appeal to me in the slightest. I am sure this policy of retaliation and vicarious punishment will ruin India as well as Pakistan.'[11] That dire prediction appears now to be coming true.

India and Pakistan may have centuries of shared history but the contending nationalisms, passionately taught in schools and also cultivated through jihadism and Hindutva extremism for sixty-nine years, have eroded the commonalities between the two people. Moreover, both countries have given priority to ideology over pragmatism in their relations. Layers of allegations and complaints have piled on over the decades. Indians are angry about Pakistan protecting the underworld figure Dawood Ibrahim, responsible for multiple bomb blasts in Mumbai in 1993, as well as about Pakistan's support for Hafiz Saeed, Masood Azhar and other jihadi militants responsible for terror attacks in India. Pakistanis blame India for stirring up rebellion and supporting separatists in Balochistan in addition to financing extremist groups in Karachi and the Khyber-Pashtunkhwa region.

Since Independence, Pakistan has sought parity with India and described resolution of the Kashmir dispute as the essential prerequisite for normal ties with its much larger neighbour. After six decades of close ties with the United States, Pakistani analysts now speak of expanding security ties with China and Russia, ostensibly to counter a US–India axis. Pakistan describes India as an existential enemy while engaging in periodic negotiations to solve bilateral problems. That dichotomy of negotiating with someone described as an existential enemy is just one example of irrationality. Another is the pursuit of equivalence. Seeking security against a much larger neighbour is a rational objective but seeking parity with it constantly is not.

The India–Pakistan equation should have changed fundamentally after both countries acquired nuclear weapons. Deterrence and mutually assured destruction usually freeze conflicts but that cannot happen if one side is ideologically committed to seeking resolution of disputes before anything else. With nuclear weapons, Pakistan does not need to feel insecure about being militarily overrun by India. The notion of an existential threat to Pakistan is now only psycho-political and ideological. Pakistan has already fought four wars with India and lost half its territory in the process, the erstwhile East Pakistan, which became Bangladesh in 1971.

There is an inherent contradiction in Pakistan's stance that India's real goal is to undo Partition but that the dispute over Jammu and Kashmir is the 'core problem' in India–Pakistan relations. There is no explanation for how and why resolution of the Kashmir dispute would stop India from wanting to undo Partition, if indeed that is what India wants. As for Jammu and Kashmir, one need not deny the sense of injustice felt by Pakistanis to point out that it might not be an issue that can be resolved in the foreseeable future. Pakistan would do better to heed Chinese President Jiang Zemin's advice and shelve it temporarily to build 'normal state-to-state relations'.

Pakistan and India could try to reduce their mutual mistrust by expanding interaction of their citizens through cultural and sports exchanges, trade and opening of travel. The Pakistan military, however, refuses to let civilian leaders pursue that path. India is as beholden to reciprocity – the idea that it will not do anything for Pakistan that Pakistan is not willing to do in return – as Pakistan is to parity. That renders impossible any prospect of India's unilateral concessions paving the way for diminishing antagonisms.

Reason would suggest that Pakistan would benefit from changing its goal from seeking parity with India to ensuring national security and economic development. Pakistan can no longer count on the United States as an equalizer in its quest to be on a par with India. China – already a close ally of Pakistan – cannot tip the balance in Pakistan's favour on its own. All nations have sovereign equality in international law but realpolitik demands acknowledgement of the difference of size between nations.

Pakistan is India's rival in real terms only as much as Belgium could rival France or Germany. India's population is six times larger than Pakistan's while its economy is ten times bigger. Notwithstanding problems of poverty and corruption (which Pakistan also faces), India's $2-trillion economy has managed consistent growth whereas Pakistan's $245-billion economy has grown only in spurts. Over time, the economic gap will only widen. Instead of resenting India, Pakistan could stake a claim to its own share of prosperity. Two-way trade between India and China stands at $72 billion even though the two countries are often considered rivals. The volume of India–Pakistan trade is a measly $2 billion.

The discord between India and Pakistan is also holding back the entire South Asian region, home to around 1.7 billion people living in eight countries – Afghanistan, Bangladesh, Bhutan, India, Maldives, Nepal, Pakistan and Sri Lanka. The combined GDP (at nominal rates) of these countries stands at $2.9 trillion and it is the least integrated region in the world. Intra-regional trade comprises only 5 per cent of the total trade of South Asia's eight countries. There are few flights between the region's capitals, and road and rail links are in poor condition or non-existent.

This is in stark comparison to the ASEAN (Association of Southeast Nations) region, home to 650 million people, ten countries and a combined GDP of $2.6 trillion, where 25 per cent of all trade involves neighbours. Half of all trade under the North American Free Trade Agreement (NAFTA) that binds Canada, the United States and Mexico takes place within the region, as it does in the European Union.

The opening of trade and the economic benefits that flow from it could help Indians and Pakistanis realize the benefit of living, as Jinnah wanted, like Canada and the United States. Joint strategies to deal with the fast-melting Himalayan glaciers, the looming water shortage in the entire subcontinent and managing the Sindh–Rajasthan desert together could be other areas of cooperation. Students from India and Pakistan could study in each other's colleges and universities, to benefit from the different strengths in varied fields that have developed on the two sides of the border. The same principle could apply to health care, with both sides opening their hospitals to each other's citizens. Once Indians and Pakistanis start dealing more with each other their similarities could re-emerge and the contrived animosities could begin to diminish.

The chances of that happening appear slim at the moment. India and Pakistan are unlikely to open their borders to each other while they suspect the other of being bent on destroying them. Students, businessmen, doctors and patients, even musicians and artists, all are seen at the moment as potential spies and even potential terrorists. For a new India–Pakistan relationship, Pakistanis would have to give up jihadi fantasies while Indians will have to stop their regression into communal fervour.

Pakistan's first military dictator, General Ayub Khan stated in his memoirs that India's argument has always been 'Let us forget our disputes; let us have a "no war pact;" let us have more trade, more freedom of movement between the two countries and more cultural freedom exchanges. This will soften feelings on the two sides and once an atmosphere of goodwill and understanding develops all problems will resolve themselves.' Ayub framed Pakistan's position as being 'to ask how goodwill and understanding can develop when basic differences and disputes remain unresolved'.

Nonetheless, India is expanding by most measures of national power while Pakistan has been able to keep pace with it only in manufacturing nuclear weapons and their delivery systems. Pakistanis are often not told of the widening gap between the two countries in most fields including education, scientific research and innovation. Pakistan vehemently opposes a permanent seat for India in the United Nations Security Council and membership of the Nuclear Suppliers Group. Pakistan cannot realistically expect either for itself but would like to deny them to India as well.

Instead of breeding competition with India in the national psyche, Pakistan could concentrate on building its democracy, eliminating terrorism, improving its infrastructure and modernizing its economy. But the competition with India continues to be nurtured in Pakistan, sometimes to absurd lengths. On the eve of the Pakistan–India match during the cricket World Cup of 2015 in Adelaide, the spokesman of the Pakistan army, Lt Gen. Asim Bajwa, tweeted, 'The whole nation stands behind our team for an astounding performance. Spirits and morale both of team & nation seems sky high.' The general did not, as a rule, tweet about cricket and remained silent during other matches of the World Cup series but felt compelled to weigh in where Pakistan's team was facing India.

Indians, too, are increasingly taking competition with Pakistan to unbelievable lengths though admittedly India's military does not play as central a role in encouraging this sentiment as Pakistan's.

Young Indians were arrested in Meerut and Aligarh in 2014 for cheering the Pakistani side during cricket matches. In October 2015, right-wing extremist Hindu nationalists doused the head of an Indian think-tank intellectual in black ink to protest his organizing the launch in Mumbai of a book by a former Pakistani foreign minister. The same month a concert by the Pakistani ghazal singer Ghulam Ali was cancelled after threats from the same radical group, which argued that the singer belonged to 'a country which is firing bullets at Indians'.[12] A firebrand Muslim politician, Asaduddin Owaisi, is being described by the Indian media as a 'new Jinnah' over his demagoguery about Hindu–Muslim divisions.

India is as ill served by some of its public figures

positing that 600 million Muslims of the subcontinent, living in Pakistan, India and Bangladesh, are all its enemies, as Pakistan is by the unrealistic, never-ending competition with India.

The India–Pakistan relationship has become a victim of two parallel and contending nationalisms. Under the military's influence, Pakistani nationalism has evolved as anti-Indianism. According to the leading Pakistani thinker Khaled Ahmed, 'Pakistani nationalism comprises 95% India hatred. They call it Islam because that is how we learn to differentiate between ourselves and India.' Indian nationalism, on the other hand, insists on describing Pakistani identity as inherently communal and constantly reiterates the need to dispute the two- nation theory. By definition this puts Pakistan down and on the defensive instead of making it feel respected and self-confident.

When Pakistanis rally around their flag, they are forced to defend the two-nation theory if it is under attack from Indians even when they would rather embrace a functional, as opposed to ideological, nationalism. Indians might better succeed in weakening the anti-India aspect of Pakistani nationalism by repeating more often Vajpayee's unequivocal acceptance of Pakistan, recorded at the Minar-e-Pakistan in Lahore. The task of debating the irrelevance of the two-nation theory in the twenty-first century should be left to Pakistanis, who cannot ignore harsh facts forever.

The Pakistani poet Fehmida Riaz, in her poem 'Tum Bilkul Hum Jaise Nikle' (Turned out you were just like us) reflects the wistfulness of secular Pakistanis who, while working for Pakistan to overcome its religious passions and fury, have ended up having to see India become more like Pakistan. The poem in Urdu has been translated into English by Shabana Mir thus:

Turned out you were just like us.

So it turned out you were just like us!

Where were you hiding all this time, buddy?

That stupidity, that ignorance

we wallowed in for a century –

look, it arrived at your shores too!

Many congratulations to you!

Raising the flag of religion,

I guess now you'll be setting up Hindu Raj?

India vs Pakistan

You too will commence to muddle everything up
You, too, will ravage your beautiful garden.
You, too, will sit and ponder –
I can tell preparations are afoot –
who is [truly] Hindu, who is not.
I guess you'll be passing fatwas soon!
Here, too, it will become hard to survive.
Here, too, you will sweat and bleed.
You'll barely make do joylessly.
You will gasp for air like us.
I used to wonder with such deep sorrow.
And now, I laugh at the idea:
it turned out you were just like us!
We weren't two nations after all!
To hell with education and learning.
Let's sing the praises of ignorance.
Don't look at the potholes in your path:
bring back instead the times of yore!
Practice harder till you master
the skill of always walking backwards.
Let not a single thought of the present
break your focus upon the past!

Repeat the same thing over and over –
over and over, say only this:
How glorious was India in the past!
How sublime was India in days gone by!
Then, dear friends, you will arrive
and get to heaven after all.
Yep. We've been there for a while now.
Once you are there,
once you're in the same hellhole,
keep in touch and tell us how it goes!

Notes

1. 'We Can Either Be More Than Friends or Become More Than Enemies'

1. Embassy Karachi to State Department, March 22, 1948. 845F.00/3-2247, Department of State Records. Cited in Dennis Kux, *Disenchanted Allies: The United States and Pakistan, 1947–2000*, Baltimore: Johns Hopkins University Press, 2001. p. 25.

2. Stanley Wolpert, *Jinnah of Pakistan*, New York: Oxford University Press, 1984. p. vii.

3. Ibid.

4. Rajmohan Gandhi, *Rajaji: A Life*, New Delhi: Penguin, 1997. pp. 247–49.

5. Muhammad Ali Jinnah's Presidential Address to the Constituent Assembly of Pakistan at Karachi, 11 August 1947.

6. I.S. Jehu (Ed.), *The Indian and Pakistan Year Book 1948*, Vol. 34, Bombay: Bennett, Coleman. p. 945. Cited in K.B. Sayeed, *Pakistan: The Formative Phase*, Ann Arbor: University of Michigan Press, 1960. p. 175.

7. *The Statesman* (Delhi), 14 June 1947.

8. Paul R. Brass, 'The Partition of India and Retributive Genocide in the Punjab, 1946–47: Means, Methods, and Purposes', *The Journal of Genocide Research* 5(1): 75; Prashant Bharadwaj, Asim Khwaja and Atif Mian, 'The Big March: Migratory Flows after the Partition of India', *Economic and Political Weekly*, 30 August 2008.

9. Jawaharlal Nehru's Speech at Aligarh University, 24 January 1948. *Jawaharlal Nehru Speeches. Sept 1946–May 1949*, Vol. 1, New Delhi: Press Publication Division, Ministry of Information and Broadcasting. pp. 337–39.

10. Ramachandra Guha, *India After Gandhi: The History*

of the World's Largest Democracy, New Delhi: Pan Macmillan, 2011. p. xiii.

11. 'Pakistan's Message to the World Is Equity, Fraternity and Justice, says Liaquat Ali', *Dawn*, 5 May 1948.

12. Abdul Ghaffar Khan and K.B. Narang. *My Life and Struggle: Autobiography of Badshah Khan*. Hind Pocket Books, 1969.

13. G.M. Syed, *The Case for Sindh: G.M. Sayed's Deposition for the Court*, Karachi: Naeen Sindh Academy, 1993.

14. O.H.K. Spate, 'The Partition of India and the Prospects of Pakistan', *Geographical Review* 38(1): 17. Table III 'Area and Population of India and Pakistan, 1941'.

15. Ayesha Jalal, *The State of Martial Rule*. p. 42.

16. 'Liaquat Asks Army for Social Service and Sacrifices', *Dawn*, 10 April 1948.

17. Muhammad Ayub Khan, *Friends Not Masters: A Political Biography*, Karachi: Oxford University Press, 1967. p. 172.

18. Ibid. p. 183.

19. Margaret Bourke-White, *Halfway to Freedom*, New York: Simon and Schuster, 1949. p. 99.

20. Huseyn Shaheed Suhrawardy, Constituent Assembly Records (Legislature), 2 March 1948. p. 136.

21. Homer A. Jack (Ed.), *The Gandhi Reader*, Bloomington: Indiana University Press, 1956. pp. 454–56.

22. Vazira Fazila Yacoobali Zamindar, *The Long Partition and the Making of Modern South Asia: Refugees, Boundaries, Histories*, New York: Columbia University Press, 2007. pp. 181–83.

23. Ibid. p. 177.

24. Note by Sir Gilbert Laithwaite, Permanent Under-secretary of State for Commonwealth Relations, on General Ayub, dated 28 October 1958, *The British Papers 1958–69*, Karachi: Oxford University Press, 2002. pp. 47–48.

25. Herbert Feldman, *From Crisis to Crisis: Pakistan, 1962-69*, London: Oxford University Press, 1972. p. 146.

26. Jawaharlal Nehru. *Speeches*, Vol. 2. p. 446.

27. Ramachandra Guha, *India After Gandhi: The History of the World's Largest Democracy*, New York: Oxford University Press, 2003. p. 400.

28. Text of President Ayub Khan's address to the nation,

6 September 1965 in Rais Ahmad Jafri (Ed.), *Ayub: Soldier and Statesman*, Lahore: Mohammad Ali Academy, 1966. pp. 138–39.

29. Abdurrahman Siddiqui, *The Military in Pakistan: Image and Reality*, Lahore: Vanguard Press, 1996, p. 107.

30. Zulfikar Ali Bhutto, *If I Am Assassinated...*, New Delhi: Vikas Publishing House, 1979. p. 130.

2. 'Kashmir Is Pakistan's Jugular Vein'

1. M.M.R. Khan, *United Nations and Kashmir*. p. 62. It is significant that the argument in Pakistan has changed little since 1955, when Khan's book was published.

2. Speech by President Jiang Zemin to the Pakistan Senate, 'Carrying Forward Friendly and Neighborly Relations from Generation to Generation, and Working Together for a Better Tomorrow', 6 December 1996. http://karachi.china-consulate.org/eng/zbgx/t263901.htm

3. Ramachandra Guha, *India After Gandhi: The History of the World's Largest Democracy*, New York: Oxford

University Press, 2003. pp. 56–57.

4. Nicholas Mansergh, et al. (Eds) *The Transfer of Power 1942-7: Constitutional Relations between Britain and India*, London: H.M. Stationery Office, 1983. Vol. 12. p. 121.

5. Ramachandra Guha, *India After Gandhi: The History of the World's Largest Democracy*, New York: Oxford University Press, 2003. pp. 78–83.

6. 'Memorandum of a Conversation between President Eisenhower and President Ayub Khan, Karachi, December 8, 1959, 9 a.m.' *FRUS, 1958-60*, Vol. 15. pp. 781–92.

7. Y.D. Gundevia, *Outside the Archives*, Pune: Sangam Books, 1984. p. 306.

8. Altaf Gauhar, 'Four Wars, One Assumption', *The Nation*, 5 September 1999.

9. Altaf Gauhar, *Ayub Khan: Pakistan's First Military Ruler*, Karachi: Oxford University Press, 1996. p. 328.

10. Lincoln P. Bloomfield, 'Peace Lessons', 13 June 2002, *Christian Science Monitor*.

11. Hilary Rodham Clinton, *Hard Choices*, New York: Simon & Schuster, 2014. p. 421.

12. Pervez Musharraf, *In the Line of Fire: A Memoir*, New York: Free Press, 2006. pp. 299–301.

13. Telegram 5434 From the Embassy in Pakistan to the Department of State, June 22, 1972, Foreign Relations of the United States, 1969–1976, Vol. E–7, Documents on South Asia, 1969–1972.

14. Ibid.

3. 'We Should Use the Nuclear Bomb'

1. Peter Landesman, 'A Modest Proposal from the Brigadier: What One Prominent Pakistani Thinks His Country Should Do with Its Atomic Weapons', *The Atlantic*, March 2002.

2. 'Nuclear Arsenal Is for the Defence of Pakistan', *The News*, 3 March 2016.

3. Feroz Hassan Khan, *Eating Grass: The Making of the Pakistani Bomb*, Stanford: Stanford University Press, 2012. pp. 2–3.

4. Abdul Qadeer Khan, 'My Nuclear Manifesto', *Newsweek*, 16 May 2011.

5. Tim McGirk and Syed Talat Hussain, 'Pakistan's

Abdul Qadeer Khan', *Time*, 30 November 1998.

6. William Langewiesche, 'The Wrath of Khan', *The Atlantic*, November 2005.

7. 'Pakistan Can Wipe Out India in Few Seconds, Says Dr Samar Mubarakmand', 92 News, 3 September 2015. http://92newshd.tv/pakistan-can-wipe-out-india-in-few-seconds-says-dr-samar-mubarak/

8. Mariana Babbar, 'European Businessmen Sold Nuclear Technology to Pakistan', *The News*, 11 April 2016.

9. Feroz Hassan Khan, *Eating Grass: The Making of the Pakistani Bomb*, Stanford: Stanford University Press, 2012. p. 6.

10. John Ward Anderson, 'Pakistan Sets Off Nuclear Blasts: Today We Have Settled a Score, Premier Says', *Washington Post*, 29 May 1998.

11. Executive Summary, 'From Surprise to Reckoning: Kargil Committee Report', July 1999.

12. Bruce Riedel, 'American Diplomacy and the 1999 Kargil Summit at Blair House', Center for the Advanced Study of India, University of Pennsylvania, 2002.

13. Walter Ladwig, 'A Cold Start for Hot Wars? The Indian Army's New Limited War Doctrine', *International Security* 32(3): 158–90.

14. 'US Embassy Cables: India "Unlikely" to Deploy Cold Start against Pakistan', *Guardian*, 30 November 2010.

15. Pervez Hoodbhoy, 'Is Third Largest Large Enough?' *Dawn*, 29 August 2015.

4. Terrorism=Irregular Warfare

1. '10 Terrorists Have Entered Gujarat: Pakistan's NSA', *Times of India*, 6 March 2016.

2. 'Raids across Gujarat, Alert Nationwide after Intelligence Inputs on Possible Terrorist Attacks', *Indian Express*, 7 March 2016.

3. Praveen Swami, 'Pakistan NSA Warned Ajit Doval of 26/11-type Hit on Maha Shivratri', *Indian Express*, 7 March 2016.

4. 'Pathankot Attack: Pakistan Wants More Leads from India, Probe Hits Dead End', Press Trust of India, Lahore, 1 February 2016.

5. Mian Abrar, 'JIT Report Pokes Holes in India's

Pathankot Theories', *Pakistan Today*, 4 April 2016.

6. 'Pathankot Probe: Pakistan JIT Didn't Contradict NIA Evidence, Say Indian Officials', Indo Asian News Service, 28 March 2016.

7. Praveen Swami, 'Pakistan NSA Warned Ajit Doval of 26/11-type Hit on Maha Shivratri', *Indian Express*, 7 March 2016.

8. Indian Fatalities, 1994–2016, South Asian Terrorism Portal, accessed 3 April 2016.

9. Fatalities in Terrorist Violence in Jammu and Kashmir, 1988–2016, South Asian Terrorism Portal, accessed 3 April 2016.

10. South Asian Terrorism Portal http://www.satp.org/

11. Sectarian Violence in Pakistan, 1989–2016, South Asian Terrorism Portal, accessed 3 April 2016.

12. M. Ayub Khan, *Asian Review*, July 1958. p. 225.

13. Aslam Siddiqui, *Pakistan Seeks Security*, Lahore: Longman & Greens, 1960. p. 67.

14. Ibid. p. 65.

15. Muhammad Yusuf and Mark Adkin, *Afghanistan: The Bear Trap: The Defeat of a Superpower*, New York: Casemate, 2001; Steve Coll, *Ghost Wars: The Secret*

History of the CIA, Afghanistan and Bin Laden, from the Soviet Invasion to September 10, 2001, New York: Penguin Books, 2004.

16. Statistical Report on General Election 1987, to the Legislative Assembly of Jammu and Kashmir, Election Commission of India website. http:// eci.nic.in/eci_main/StatisticalReports/SE_1987/ StatisticalReport_jk_87.pdf

17. Major General M. Amin Khan Burki, In Foreword to Lt. Colonel Javed Hassan, *India: A Study in Profile*, Rawalpindi: Services Book Club, 1990. p. ii.

18. Ibid. p. 111.

19. Ibid. p. 139.

20. Letter from Secretary of State James A. Baker III to Prime Minister Nawaz Sharif, 10 May 1992.

21. Reply from Prime Minister Nawaz Sharif to Secretary of State James Baker, 20 June 1992.

22. October 1992, Pakistan's ISID paper on India's Research and Analysis Wing.

23. 'Duplicitous, a Gentler Way to Describe ISI: Ex-CIA Chief', Press Trust of India, 24 February 2016.

5. The Space for Friendship Is Shrinking

1. Michael T. Kaufman, 'Pakistan's Islamic Revival Affects All Aspects of Life', *New York Times*, 13 October 1980.

2. Waheed-uz-Zaman, *The Quest for Identity* (Proceedings of The First Congress on the History and Culture of Pakistan, April 1973) Islamabad: University of Islamabad Press, 1974. p. i.

3. Speech delivered by Zulfikar Ali Bhutto at the UN Security Council on 22 September 1965, http://www.bhutto.org/1957-1965_speech21.php

4. Cited in Michael Brecher, *India and World Politics: Krishna Menon's View of the World*, New York: Oxford University Press, 1968. pp. 170–71.

5. J.N. Dixit, *India–Pakistan in War & Peace*, London: Routledge Publishers, 2002. p. 7.

6. K.K. Aziz, *The Murder of History in Pakistan*, Lahore: Vanguard Books, 1993. p. 1.

7. Ibid. pp. 188–205.

8. Ibid. p. 227.

9. Farahnaz Ispahani, *Purifying the Land of the Pure*, New Delhi: HarperCollins India, 2016.

10. Darshan Desai, 'As per Gujarat School Textbooks, Japan Nuked US', *India Today*, 17 June 2014.

11. Nehru to Patel, 20 February 1950, SPC, Vol. 10. p. 5. Cited in Ramachandra Guha, *India After Gandhi: The History of the World's Largest Democracy*, New York: Oxford University Press, 2003. p. 241.

12. Alok Deshpande, 'Ghulam Ali Concert Called Off after Shiv Sena Threats', *The Hindu*, 8 October 2015.

A Note on the Author

A former Pakistani ambassador to the US, Husain Haqqani has also been a journalist, academic and adviser to four Pakistani prime ministers, including Benazir Bhutto. He is the author of *Pakistan: Between Mosque and Military* and *Magnificent Delusions: US, Pakistan and an Epic History of Misunderstanding*. He is currently Director for South and Central Asia at the Hudson Institute in Washington DC.

juggernaut

THE APP FOR INDIAN READERS

Fresh, original books tailored for mobile and for India. Starting at ₹10.

juggernaut.in

CRAFTED
FOR MOBILE
READING

Thought you would never read a book on mobile? Let us prove you wrong.

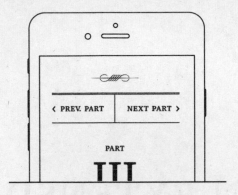

Beautiful Typography

The quality of print transferred
to your mobile. Forget ugly PDFs.

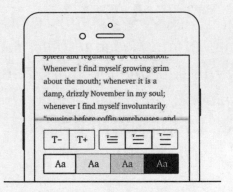

Customizable Reading

Read in the font size, spacing
and background of your liking.

AN EXTENSIVE LIBRARY

Including fresh, new, original Juggernaut books from the likes of Sunny Leone, Praveen Swami, Husain Haqqani, Umera Ahmed, Rujuta Diwekar and lots more. Plus, books from partner publishers and loads of free classics. Whichever genre you like, there's a book waiting for you.

DON'T JUST READ; INTERACT

Thought you would never read a book on mobile? Let us prove you wrong.

Ask authors questions

Get all your answers from the horse's mouth.
Juggernaut authors actually reply to every
question they can.

Rate and review

Let everyone know of your favourite reads or
critique the finer points of a book – you will be
heard in a community of like-minded readers.

Gift books to friends

For a book-lover, there's no nicer gift than
a book personally picked. You can even
do it anonymously if you like.

Enjoy new book formats

Discover serials released in parts over
time, picture books including comics,
and story-bundles at discounted rates.
And coming soon, audiobooks.

LOWEST PRICES & ONE-TAP BUYING

Books start at ₹10 with regular discounts and free previews.

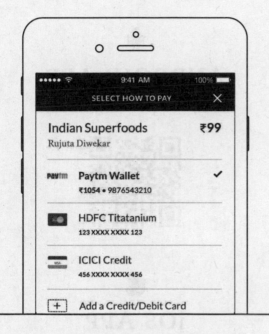

Paytm Wallet and Cards

Just connect your Paytm Wallet (or create one)
once and buy any book with one tap. Or pay
with your debit or credit card.

Click the QR Code with a QR scanner app
or type this link into the Internet browser
on your phone to download the app.

ANDROID APP

bit.ly/juggernautandroid

iOS APP

bit.ly/juggernautios

For our complete catalogue, visit www.juggernaut.in
To submit your book, send a synopsis and two
sample chapters to books@juggernaut.in
For all other queries, write to contact@juggernaut.in

ENG-7